COACHING
MADE EASY

Praise for **Coaching Made Easy**

"It is easy to lose sight of the fact that sustainable results can only be achieved through others. Equally, this can rarely be accomplished without effective coaching from leaders. Effective coaching not only achieves outcomes, but also facilitates talent development. Why isn't this done more often? Leaders lack the playbook for effective coaching. Finally, in *Coaching Made Easy*, we have the COACH framework that is accessible to all who are committed: **C**ommunicate, **O**pen, **A**lign, **C**ollaborate and **H**arness. With many realistic examples and articulation of supporting behaviors, this is the 'how to' book that will help leaders facilitate great individual and organizational effectiveness. I cannot recommend it more highly!"

– Joseph R. Bongiovi,
Chief Human Resources Officer, Sazerac Company, Inc.

"*Coaching Made Easy* presents a five-part framework that is easy to understand and apply. I love the examples that are shared in each part of the coaching framework—it is easy to see how those everyday examples translate to my work environment. Alonzo does a great job of weaving in the different behaviors related to each element of the framework. I believe leaders at all levels can benefit from these insights."

– Martha Trott,
Vice President, Human Resources, Americas, DeLaval

"This book is not only great if you have just started coaching or considering it, but invaluable for seasoned veterans. The content is actionable the *first time* you read it. I found myself nodding my head throughout each section. I am grateful to have been brought back to the basics of coaching."

– Robin Mottern,
Executive Coach, Emotional Intelligence Practitioner

"I'm a trained coach and mentor, but rarely have I come across a book on coaching that is straight forward, practical and easy to apply. *Coaching Made Easy* is a concise practical guide that I will recommend to my students and clients who are dealing with real-world challenges. Dr. Alonzo's many years of experience in coaching others successfully are evident in each section of this book."

–Musa Nyakora, Ph.D.,
Professor of OD and Leadership Programs, Adventist University of Africa

COACHING
MADE EASY

**A Framework for
Enhancing Performance**

Alonzo Johnson, Ph.D.

OASYS Press ◊ McDonough, GA

Coaching Made Easy
A Framework for Enhancing Performance

Copyright © 2019 by OASYS Press. All rights reserved. No part of this book may be reproduced or transmitted in any form or by any means, electronic or mechanical, including photocopying, recording or by any information storage and retrieval system, without written permission from the author, except for the inclusion of brief quotations in a review.

This book is designed to provide information about effective coaching. It is sold with the understanding that the publisher and author make no representations or warranty with respect to the accuracy or completeness of the content contained herein, and disclaim any implied warranties of merchantability or fitness for a particular purpose. The content of this book may not be suitable for your situation. If expert assistance is required, the services of a competent professional should be sought. The author and publisher shall have neither liability nor responsibility to any person or entity with respect to any loss or damage caused, or alleged to have been caused, directly or indirectly, by the information contained in this book.

Printed in the United States of America
First Edition, 2019

21 20 19 18 17 16 15 1 2 3 4 5

978-0-9863965-6-4 (paperback)
978-0-9863965-7-1 (e-book)

Visit the author's websites:
www.AlonzoJohnsonPHD.com
www.TheOASYSGroup.com

Cover design by Daniel Swanson and Tyora Moody
Book layout by Darlene K. Swanson

◊ ◊ ◊ ◊ ◊

Coaching Made Easy is available for sale at special quantity discounts. For more information, please visit AlonzoJohnsonPHD.com, or email inquiries to Alonzo@TheOASYSGroup.com.

THE **MADE EASY** SERIES

HIRING
MADE EASY AS PIE

LEADING
MADE EASY

COACHING
MADE EASY

ASYS Press

CONTENTS

Acknowledgement 5
Preface 7
Introduction 9

COMMUNICATE   19

OPEN   61

ALIGN   89

COLLABORATE   125

HARNESS   149

Conclusion 169
Suggested Readings 171
About the Author 173
About The OASYS Group 175

ACKNOWLEDGEMENT

According to Michele Milan, "We are creatures of habit, and from our habits we create ourselves, our lives and the world around us." To those who worked alongside me and helped me develop the habits necessary to complete this book, I am forever grateful!

I am especially grateful to Annmarie Buchanan for sharing my vision for the COACH framework presented in this book and contributing content to support it.

I also acknowledge Professor Joseph Petrosko, Emeritus, for helping with the statistical analyses and validation of the behaviors underpinning the elements of the COACH framework.

To Frances Paschall, Jeffrey Corkran, and Jim Ehlers who helped with initial editing and organizing of this book, and Steve Schultz, President of Writing at Work, who spent countless hours making final edits—a heartfelt thank you.

To those I have coached over the years, your trust inspired me to develop the COACH framework. Thank you for believing and allowing me to grow as a coach.

PREFACE

Influencing team members to achieve high levels of performance and build capacity for future organizational success is probably the most important task that leaders perform. Coaching is arguably the most effective tool that leaders have to accomplish that task. When done properly, coaching can help others to assess their skills and determine how to broaden them. It can also help others to recognize and eliminate unproductive behaviors. Given all its benefits, it's safe to conclude that coaching is indispensable for leaders to help team members excel professionally and personally, while maintaining the overall health of their organizations

Effective coaching is a critical need at every level of the organization; however, most leaders don't take the time to do it or don't do it well. This may be due to misunderstanding of what coaching is, its benefits or how to do it effectively. It could also be that leaders are apprehensive about coaching their team members because there is no script in coaching, and every person is unique with different needs.

Regardless of the reason, effective coaching remains perhaps the most valuable, yet underutilized people-development tool in organizations. Anyone who is in a leadership role has to be comfortable with coaching team members at any time, whenever it is needed. Coaching may take place between a frontline supervisor (who plays the role of coach) and a direct report (the person receiving the coaching), but coaching relationships can and do exist at different levels of organizations and within a much larger context. Regardless of the organizational strata in which coaching takes place, quality coaching cannot occur in a vacuum; the right foundation has to be built. Leaders who are responsible for charting the strategic course for their organizations have to be intentional about developing a coaching culture. They do this to continuously unleash the untapped potential of their workforce in order to remain relevant to customers and stakeholders. To truly be effective, every leader in the organization must understand what coaching is, the value it brings and how to develop the right coaching behaviors.

This book presents a framework that anyone can use to coach others towards excellence. While it is essential for everyone to have the skills to coach effectively, a leader is required to have the right skills to coach team members effectively. This book provides a framework for coaching your team members so that they can achieve their performance, professional or personal goals and move the organization forward. The COACH framework will expose you to effective coaching behaviors that, when practiced, will lead to effective coaching relationships.

INTRODUCTION

> *"Coaching is unlocking a person's potential to maximize their own performance. It is helping them to learn rather than teaching them."*
>
> — Timothy Gallwey

So, are you a coach?

Have you ever been coached?

Before you answer those questions, let's briefly discuss two terms: coach and protégé.

A coach helps others to accomplish their goals. A protégé, sometimes called a coachee, receives guidance or support from a coach to accomplish goals. In an organizational context, a protégé would be a team member who receives guidance from a supervisor to fulfill a goal.

Perhaps the most vivid example of a coach is in sports. Think of sport coaches you have worked with or observed over a period of time. These coaches don't play the games; they strategize and offer guidance to team members before, during and after games to win games and championships. Some of the best coaches are highly sought after and handsomely rewarded.

So, are you a coach or a protégé?

The answer is you are both—coach and protégé.

Regardless of whether you have a formal leadership title or are in a position of power, you have likely assumed the role of coach and protégé at some point in your life.

Think about your physical growth and development. Your parents or caregivers played various roles throughout the stages of your development journey. They likely coached you through taking your first step, to saying your first words, to reading and writing. You likely graduated to riding a bike, then to driving a car, selecting a career path, and so on.

In all of life's milestones, if you think about it, someone was likely there providing you with guidance and influencing your decisions. You were a protégé. You may sometimes think fondly of those people who were there for you as role models, rather than coaches; but undoubtedly some coaching took place during those formative years. Then, as you accomplished those milestones, you gained enough experience to begin influencing and guiding the decisions of others by performing a number of roles—including playing the role of coach. You may have found yourself encouraging an infant's first step, first words, or later, helping a recent graduate prepare for the first job interview. On the job, you may have helped a coworker become more confident in performing a task. Not all of those roles will be considered coaching in its purest sense, but you may have unwittingly coached others to improve their performance or accomplish a goal.

So if the world is filled with coaches and protégés, why is there such a dearth of effective coaching relationships within organizations? Why do organizational leaders invest in executive level coaching but often fall short on a strategy for building and sustaining a coaching culture?

Could it be that these leaders realize that coaching is a valuable tool that is not being deployed effectively, if at all, in the organization? Could it be that organizational leaders' remedy for this deficit is to employ coaching at the highest leadership levels in hopes that its benefits would trickle down to every team member?

The lack of an effective organization-wide coaching system, however, creates a never-ending demand for one. How well an organization deploys coaching will determine the level of its overall success.

Let me explain. The term coaching has taken on different meanings in organizations. Some leaders would pass a coaching polygraph test and be surprised to learn that they are not coaching anyone. Think of this scenario: Jamie is a good worker. Lately he has been making mistakes on the job. Although Jamie has gotten the resources to be successful, the poor performance has continued. Jamie's manager has decided to coach him.

What does coaching mean to you in this situation? Are you thinking that Jamie's manager will be pointing out the shortcomings and asking Jamie to improve his performance or face consequences?

If you are, then you are thinking like a lot of people. Many people think of coaching as constructive criticism, a reprimand or negative feedback—it is none of these. An organization cannot build a successful coaching culture if there is no consensus on what coaching is and how it should be deployed.

Let's spend some more time with the term coaching. Coaching is a vehicle or tool to help people get from where they are to where they want to be. Coaching is a leadership practice that allows a leader to intellectually stimulate and motivate team members. It builds trust, enhances team members' capacity, boosts morale and confidence, as well as strengthens team cohesiveness. In the workplace, a leader coaches team members so that they can develop skills to overcome challenges on their own in order to meet and exceed performance expectations.

Coaching is not telling others what to do; rather, it is encouraging others to find solutions. Effective coaches are perceived as good sounding boards, who listen attentively to others to help guide their decision-making. As a leader, your responsibility is to maintain proficient coaching skills and use them to develop others and move your organization forward.

We have determined that coaching is not about giving negative feedback. It is an opportunity to help guide your team member through a process of identifying how to develop the skills to realize on-the-job performance, personal, professional, and ultimately, organizational goals. Coaching has other misnomers. It is sometimes used interchangeably with the term mentoring. Mentoring relationships usually involve a more experienced person (the mentor) helping a less experienced person (the mentee) to realize personal or professional aspirations. For example, a novice teacher, who aspires to become a principal, may seek out an experienced principal as a mentor. In this case, the mentor can use coaching as a means of helping the teacher accomplish that career goal. Mentors usually do not supervise the work of the people they mentor, so the relationship is power-neutral. As stated, in organizations, coaching typically takes place between a manager, who plays the role of coach and a direct report or team member, who receives the coaching.

Coaching is not a performance appraisal or evaluation, but it may be used after an evaluation to help team members improve skills. In Jamie's case, coaching should not be viewed as something that is going to be given to him. It is a tool that the manager can use to help Jamie to identify the cause of the performance problem and find ways to solve it.

The ultimate goal of coaching when you are in a leadership role is to develop team members so that they can operate independently and become self-sufficient. Coaching is one of the best ways to demonstrate your leadership skills.

As the saying goes, there is a time and place for everything. Coaching should take place at the right time to the right team member for the right reasons. A leader should not only know how to coach, but also when to coach. Let's discuss when coaching is required. Typically, coaching occurs when a team member knows how to perform a task or accomplish a goal, but lacks confidence, motivation, or both. As a coach, your duty is to empower team members to accomplish goals by influencing them to act. You will coach team members when performance is below standard, when they seek you out for coaching, or when there is a need to set performance goals. Remember, both the coach and team member or protégé must know what needs to be accomplished and what success looks like. Coaching is an empowering experience for your team members and will motivate them to excel. In addition, it can build trust because you are demonstrating that you trust them to solve problems on their own.

Are you creating a coaching-friendly work environment in which team members find purpose in what they do and constantly seek out growth opportunities?

Let's get back to the Jamie scenario. If you were Jamie's manager and observed performance issues, how would you handle the situation?

You would provide redirective feedback to Jamie about your performance concerns and then open the door to coaching him in order to foster the desired work behavior. Let's see what redirective feedback and a coaching door opener would look like in this scenario with Jamie's manager, Paul.

Paul: Jamie, I appreciate the work you've been doing on the team. We could not have met our targets last month without your contribution. We have looked at the data and noticed that the error rates have increased in your area. We took a closer look and noticed that your error rates are higher than everyone else's on your team. I assigned someone from another team to help improve the numbers, but the error rates are not decreasing.

With this number of errors, we will likely get the attention of my boss, and we don't want that to happen. I know you like this shift. If I cannot get the rates down, I may have to assign you to another shift where I can offer more supervision. Tell me what is happening.

In this example, Jamie's manager provided redirective feedback. The manager acknowledged Jamie's contribution to the team, explained the problem from a data-driven perspective, and outlined what the possible consequences would be if performance does not improve. There is no coaching in this example. Using the words, "tell me what is happening," opens the door to a possible coaching session.

It cannot be over emphasized that to be an effective coach, a leader has to be intentional about learning how to coach effectively. Leaders cannot use Google to find a coaching script for every coachable moment that they will encounter. A number of coaching models can help leaders to structure their coaching discussions. However, being an effective coach starts with a mindset that translates to certain behaviors. Coaching Made Easy provides a framework that leaders can use to get into that mindset and guide their coaching behaviors. The framework is based on the acronym COACH and espouses five elements that leaders, including myself, have relied on over the years to coach effectively regardless of the environment: **C**ommunicate, **O**pen, **A**lign, **C**ollaborate and **H**arness. My hope is that each element and associated behaviors will provide focus to leaders and help them hone their coaching skills to create and maintain a high performing work environment.

THE MADE EASY SERIES

Coaching Made Easy is the third book in a series of self-help books designed to present simple approaches to help overcome leadership and other workplace challenges. The first book, *Hiring Made Easy as PIE*, is primarily for managers with little hiring experience. It presents a straightforward approach for interviewing and selecting best-fit employees. The second book, *Leading Made Easy*, explores how to lead effectively after the hiring process is over, and is intended for anyone desiring to build or improve leadership skills. *Coaching Made Easy* targets one of the most challenging aspects of leadership, coaching, and condenses it into a five-element framework with effective coaching behaviors.

WHO SHOULD READ THIS BOOK

This book is intended for anyone desiring to build or improve coaching skills. The five elements of the coaching framework presented in this book can be scaled and used at any type and level of an organization.

HOW TO USE THIS BOOK

Coaching Made Easy is written in an easy-to-read format and with easy-to-understand terms and concepts. There are three options for navigating this book:

1. Read it from cover to cover.
2. Read only the element you need to enhance your knowledge.
3. Review any part of it as a reference.

An end-of-section reflection activity is included for each element. The activity provides an opportunity for you to informally assess the degree to which you use the elements and behaviors presented in this book.

For a more comprehensive evaluation, a companion coaching assessment *(COACH¹⁸⁰)* is also available. The COACH¹⁸⁰ allows multiple raters (self and others) to measure your effectiveness as a coach by assessing the degree to which you use the behaviors associated with the five elements. Additional information about the COACH¹⁸⁰ is at www.AlonzoJohnsonPHD.com.

COMMUNICATE

To effectively communicate, we must realize that we are all different in the way we perceive the world and use this understanding as a guide to our communication with others.

— Anthony Robbins

This book presents a five-element framework for effective coaching: communicating, opening oneself to building and maintaining effective coaching relationships, seeking alignment on outcomes, collaborating to accomplish goals, and harnessing skills and talents of the person being coached.

If you had to select one element that is critical to the deployment of all the other elements, which element would that be?

The first element, communicate, is the standard bearer for all the other elements. You cannot build *open* interpersonal relationships, *align* with team members, *collaborate* or *harness* their skills if you are not communicating effectively. Effective communication is perhaps the most important skill that is used in any coaching relationship.

Some leaders are naturally great communicators, while others have to learn how to communicate effectively. Nelson Mandela, with powerful verbal and nonverbal communication, helped heal a country that was divided by apartheid. Through successful communication, Mandela became known and celebrated worldwide as a unifying figure. During his years of imprisonment, Mandela developed an unbreakable friendship with a prison guard, whose life was shaped by a hardline attitude of the white Afrikaner. Undoubtedly, Mandela coached this young man and influenced the way he thought about the issue of their day, apartheid.

We have no shortage of modern-day charismatic communicators. They can be found in churches, branches of government, business and everyday life. What is it about motivational speakers like Zig Ziglar and Anthony Robbins that cause people to gather to hear them speak? Nowadays, people tune in to TED Talks for nuggets of wisdom to help them through the day. Speakers from modern and historic times understand the power of effective communication and use that to influence their audiences.

As a leader, you might not be able to command an audience like a motivational speaker, but your communication skills must be developed enough for you to be successful in your role, especially when you find yourself in uncharted territories coaching your team members. You simply cannot become an effective coach if you are not accomplished at communicating with your team members. Effective coaching depends on being able to communicate effectively, not the other way around. Communicating effectively is not something that a leader does periodically with a few team members. A good leader has to communicate effectively with every team member, every time there is a need or an opportunity to do so.

So what is communication? Communication of any kind requires sending and receiving information. If you are not able to send the right messages the right way, then you are not communicating effectively. If you are not able to focus and listen effectively to the messages you are receiving and ask questions to clarify information, you are not communicating effectively. Lack of proper communication leads to false starts to any coaching relationship you intend to create.

Let's discuss what is required to communicate effectively, especially in a coaching relationship.

In coaching, communicating effectively means *listening attentively* to team members by *giving your full attention* to *help guide their decisions*. To be an effective coach, you have to create an environment in which others are encouraged and feel comfortable *communicating openly* with you and each other. An effective coach *withholds judgment, seeks clarity and gets all the facts before making a decision*. Additionally, an effective coach *provides honest feedback* and is perceived *as a good sounding board*.

Now let's spend some time exploring these behaviors.

ACTIVE LISTENING

Active listening, also known as attentive listening, is paramount in a coaching relationship. You know that you are actively listening to someone when you find yourself tuned into the words as well as the nonverbal cues accompanying those words. Have you heard the expression, *hanging on to every word?* Active listening requires you to silence your mind and focus on what the person is saying and doing. Think of a captivating movie that you have seen lately. Do you remember how focused you were on what was happening on the screen and what was being said? Were you enthralled by even the soundtracks that accompanied the movie? That is a sign that you were focused on the movie and everything else became secondary to your attention. The movie in which you were so entranced went on without any feedback from you. In fact, you may actually detest it when someone provides commentary during an attention-grabbing movie; however, actively listening does not only involve focusing on words and deeds of the person. It involves providing the right cues to let the person you are communicating with know you are listening. An effective way to demonstrate you are listening is paraphrasing, like, "So you mean ..." or use prompts, like "Go on..." "I'm listening..." to encourage communication and let the team member know you are tuned in.

Giving full attention as we listen can be a difficult skill to master in today's world because most people tend to value the ability to multi-task. Actually, there is no such thing as multi-tasking. Psychologists have proven that the brain can only focus exclusively on one thing at a time. The best you can hope for is to be able to juggle or switch seamlessly from one task to the next.

Communicate

In Western culture, listening involves making eye contact with the team member and responding both verbally and non-verbally, while listening attentively. Let team members know that what they are saying is important and has value to you and the organization. To master the ability to listen attentively, coaches must be aware of and overcome barriers that may interfere with the ability to listen actively. For example, cultural differences between the coach and the team member may be evident in the use of language, tone, facial expressions, eye contact and personal space. These differences may impede the ability to listen actively. When you listen actively, you show respect for team members' culture and contributions.

Even when you are listening, you are communicating verbally and non-verbally. In a coaching relationship, ensure that your verbal and nonverbal cues are aligned. If you are not able to send the right message to your team member because you are distracted, tired, or busy, delay the conversation.

So why is it important to give full attention and listen actively in a coaching relationship?

As a coach, your goal is to help guide your team member's decisions. The first step in doing so is to give your full attention and listen actively. Coaching is a leadership task that will be judged by your past behavior. You will not be perceived as a good coach or leader if you have not established a record of giving team members your full attention and listening to them. To be effective, you should be able to listen objectively by divesting yourself of your personal feelings and values while you are in the coaching space with your team member. You are being objective when you withhold judgment and seek to understand by asking questions and seeking clarification and, most importantly, focus on the facts that are being presented to you.

Actively listening is not just beneficial to a coach but also to the team member. Listening is essential to building and maintaining good working relationships and creating an atmosphere in which team members feel unguarded about expressing themselves in thoughts and deeds. Freedom of expression encourages autonomy, promotes sensible risk-taking and boosts morale—fuel for workplace productivity and job satisfaction.

UNDERSTANDING MENTAL MODELS

As a coach, you are still a human being with thoughts, feelings, beliefs, and attitude about everything. When you were born, you began having experiences and learning from them. Your brain began deciphering and compartmentalizing every aspect of your life, and as you grew, you began to develop what are known as *mental models*. These are like filing cabinets in the brain for everything that your senses have detected. You search the brain's filing cabinet and retrieve information on how to feel about and address each stimulus presented to you.

How can you resist the urge to interject, based on your mental models when you are coaching a team member?

It basically boils down to this: You are in a leadership position to serve your team members by playing a coaching role. You will serve by being aware of and quieting the natural inclinations that come about as a result of your mental models. An effective coach is one who will listen attentively to all of the facts and not jump to conclusions, garner preconceived notions about what someone is thinking or feeling, or hear the expected rather than what is actually said.

You are being a communicative coach when you seek clarity throughout a coaching relationship. The spoken word often gets lost because the brain is not able to process all of the information that comes in from the senses. Some information will be lost; seeking clarification is a good way to recapture that information.

ASKING QUESTIONS

Perhaps the best way to seek clarity is to ask questions. An effective coach is not one with a reservoir of answers that team members access every time they have questions or concerns. Asking questions is a powerful tool that will encourage team members to find solutions and empower them to take on challenges. When you ask the questions, you may already know the answer. Resist the urge to give it. Allow the team member to think about the answer without interfering. Ask one question at a time and listen.

There are many ways to ask questions. My first book, *Hiring Made Easy as PIE*, contains a variety of question types and they are also relevant within the coaching context. You may ask open-ended or closed-ended questions during a coaching moment. Open-ended questions require a little more input from the team member. For example, "How did you do that?" "Why do you think so? "Can you please explain…?" Closed-ended questions require a Yes or No answer. For example, "What is…?" or "How many…?"

Which type of question is better suited for coaching?

Although closed-ended questioning is necessary in coaching relationships, open-ended questions are better suited for coaching conversations. Open-ended questions help to stir critical thinking and put the responsibility on the team members to find solutions on their own.

Earlier, we discussed mental models as thoughts, motives, values, and attitudes that you and others have adopted based on life experiences. Your team member, who is engaging with you in a coaching conversation, also has mental models. Your mental model may be different from those of your team member. Open-ended questions are great for gauging your team member's thought process.

Let's say your team member has expressed interest in taking on additional responsibilities but is concerned about how her family life will be impacted. What is the first thing you think about when the team member expresses concerns about impact on the family? You might be thinking that the team member has a husband, kids and maybe even elderly parents to take care of and does not want to take time away from them. The team member might actually be thinking about her elderly pets that are living with her. Pets are usually not immediately thought of as family members. There is no room for assumptions, especially in a coaching relationship.

So how would you as a coach respond in this scenario?

To ensure that there is no misunderstanding, you should acknowledge the team member and express confidence in her work and ability to take on extra duties. You may ask her to share what her concerns are about taking on extra duties in order to understand what aspect of her family life will be impacted. Open-ended questions act as a door opener to a coaching conversation and help you gain greater insights into the personality, motivations, and other qualities of the team member that may not be immediately evident.

Probing questions work well in a coaching relationship. As the name implies, probing questions allow the coach to explore statements or responses from the team member to gain greater understanding. In a coaching discourse, it is important to help team members explore their feelings, decisions and conclusions. Probing questions provide a richer and deeper foundation on which to build an effective coaching relationship. Open-ended and probing questions are beneficial to both the coach and team member.

Effective coaches develop proper techniques for asking appropriate questions. Not only must they be open-ended and probing, they must also be non-judgmental and non-leading. Non-judgmental questions communicate openness and trust. Non-leading questions encourage the team member to explore possibilities, rather than being led to the coach's "right" answer. When a question is non-leading, there cannot be a wrong answer.

Pay attention to body language and tone of voice as much as to the words that are being spoken. Body language and tone of voice do convey messages that may be interpreted as judgmental or leading. For example, are your arms crossed or perched on your hips? Are you nodding your head while asking the team member a question? Do you respond in a curt manner when the team member raises a topic or talks about another colleague? Everything communicates; so, be aware of the non-verbal messages that you send or that you "read" when you are coaching team members.

So what are other examples of an open-ended and probing coaching question? Below are additional examples of open-ended and probing coaching questions. Although these questions are valuable in a coaching relationship, they can also become leading and judgmental as shown in the table.

Open ended	Probing	Is it Leading?	Is it Judgmental?
"Why do you feel that way?"	"Say more about that."	No	No
"How did you arrive at that conclusion?"	"You said…. I want to explore that statement."	No	No
"How would you describe…?"	"Let's spend some time with that statement."	No	No
"If you had X, what would you do?"	"Help me understand more.…"	No	No
"I think you are too young for that position. How will you ever be able to convince anyone you are ready for that role?"	"It's hard to imagine you working in sales; that is just not your personality style. Tell me more about why you think you'll make the cut."	Yes	Yes

In the table's example, an open-ended question is represented in a leading and judgmental manner. The coach is putting forward an opinion about why the team member would not be successful in the role by pointing to age. In the probing example, personality is used to cast doubt in the mind of the team member who is considering a sales position. Opinions have no place in a coaching environment unless they are requested. And when an opinion is requested, it should be presented in a non-biased manner. Pointing out physical attributes, personality or otherwise inherent characteristics of a team member usually takes a coaching encounter down a precarious path that may alienate the team member, and the coach's credibility may not recover.

So how does a coach interject opinions without negatively impacting a coaching relationship?

Well, although you are asked to provide an opinion, the opinion should be based on experience or some tangible data. Let's look at the two previous leading and judgmental examples. You might feel that a team member may not be ready for the role based on the job description or the breadth of experience the role requires. The role may have required the incumbent to have significant years of experience, well beyond the level of experience of the team member. In that case, you should point to the data and have a conversation with the team member. Ask open-ended and probing questions to allow the team member to reflect on the information that you have presented and make a decision on whether to pursue the goal or refocus. Again, if the team member requests your opinion, share it in a non-biased manner. Use objective, verifiable data, not your mental models, as a basis for your opinion in order to point out the realities.

Communicating in a coaching environment is no different from communicating in everyday situations. A coach who is aware of mental models and asks the right open-ended questions will still encounter barriers that can impede the encoding and decoding phases of communication. In the normal communication process, the message is sent and has to be understood for the feedback or response to be given. The feedback then has to be understood by the sender of the message.

The possibility is high that there will be misunderstanding during the communication process. Environmental, generational, cultural and personality filters can interfere with the message from the coach or from the team member. Additionally, depending on interest, people typically hear and comprehend about 30 percent of the information they receive. Misunderstandings can be costly, especially in a coaching relationship. After all, a coaching relationship is based on trust. Misinterpreting or misunderstanding communication during a single coaching session can derail trust and confidence; therefore, it is critical that you confirm what you have heard by restating it. Say what you've heard in your own words and have the speaker confirm that you got it right. For example, "So, I understand that you will start using the newly installed software to reduce invoice errors. Is that right?"

When you give information, have listeners confirm that they have an understanding of your message by paraphrasing what they heard. For example, "What are the action steps that we've discussed?" Always paraphrase to confirm that the message has been received and understood. This does not mean that team members have to paraphrase everything you say, but you want to make sure that they understand the salient components of the information that they've received.

COACHING THROUGH MENTAL MODELS

The mental models discussed earlier noted how they impact our view of everything in the world. In a coaching relationship, it is important to understand your team member's point of view, even if you don't agree with it. Remember, coaching is not as much about you as it is about taking your team members from where they are and guiding them to their desired destination. Your role is not to engage in debate about what you believe as opposed to what the team member believes. As discussed earlier, it is essential to maintain a non-judgmental stance throughout the entire coaching experience. As a coach, remind yourself to remain neutral and not to quickly insert opinions or try to convince the team member why your idea is better than the team member's or others involved in the coaching relationship. Your team member will work more independently and with confidence when she comes up with an idea, presents it to you, and gets balanced feedback or guidance in the form of carefully crafted, non-leading or judgmental questions for her to think critically and modify her plan of action.

Your ability to remain open to understanding different vantage points or perspectives will improve your skill as a coach. Doing so allows you to step outside yourself, your mental models, and meet team members where they are. Your goal is to guide team members to choose the best path forward to arrive at the best possible solution.

Although you may be experienced in more areas than your team member, you likely will be confronted with unfamiliar topics. This is especially true if your team member has a different cultural or generational background.

So how do you respond when a team member presents a topic that is not in your wheelhouse, and still maintain your credibility as a coach?

We learned that being an effective coach requires trust. It may become a little tricky for you, who is trusted and seen as a source of knowledge, should you find yourself in unfamiliar territory with someone who is looking to you for guidance. In this situation, you have at least three options: provide guidance based on your limited knowledge of the area, reveal your unfamiliarity with the topic and explore other sources that might be helpful, or dissuade your team member from pursuing the idea.

Which path would you choose?

Let's put this into context. Let's assume that your team member has approached you with an idea to build a streaming channel that features the company's products with consumer-related information that is not readily available to the general public. Your team member is a technology major in college and knows how to accomplish the task, but you are clueless about who to even contact in the company to pitch this idea. Do you start with the IT department, marketing, public relations, or legal?

Which path would your conversation take with the team member?

It is your duty as a coach to embrace new ideas. The world is constantly changing, and you do not have a monopoly of knowledge on everything, even if you try to keep abreast of all the latest developments. You cannot be effective if you are not open to considering new ideas and tailoring your communication to reflect that openness to help your team member to find solutions. As discussed earlier, your duty is to improve the performance of your team member and ultimately the organization. Coaching is the vehicle through which you will propel the organization forward.

Organizations remain current by being open to new ideas. Leaders who discourage or derail new ideas because of personal misgivings or lack of knowledge are doing their organizations a disservice. Remember Kmart, Sears, and Circuit City? These and numerous other well-known retailers are closing their doors or have already done so because of changing shopping trends. People no longer shop like they used to do. Instead of walking through crowded malls, more and more people now shop online.

So, keep up with new ideas that when acted on will allow your organization to adapt not only to stay competitive, but to grow. We can all expand our minds if we allow ourselves to be creative and open to change. Explore new ideas and encourage your team members to keep pace as the world changes.

You have likely had a moment to think about the options that were presented in the last scenario. Which option would you choose?

As a coach, you will listen attentively to the idea, ask thought-provoking questions, and perhaps, communicate openly about your lack of knowledge about the topic and open up channels for your team member to explore ideas. Being honest about your knowledge, skills and areas of expertise will not undermine your position as a coach; it will enhance it. Lying or misrepresenting yourself erodes trust. We have all heard that honesty is the best policy; this is especially true in a coaching relationship. It is also a good way to help build a great coaching relationship. A great organization should have an atmosphere in which the coach and the team member feel comfortable about being truthful with each other. Respectful and honest communication is critical to any organization, and it builds richer and more beneficial coaching relationships.

Let's discuss the role feedback plays in effective communication.

GIVING AND RECEIVING FEEDBACK

Another important part of communication is feedback. What does the receiver have to say after the information is received? Will it be something positive or negative? What response will you provide after you receive the message? And based on that feedback, will the team member gain or lose confidence in you or the coaching relationship?

Feedback does not only exist as a component of simple day-to-day communication; it occurs in a larger context. Feedback is communication that provides information about what we need to stop doing, start doing or continue doing. An effective coach should know how to provide feedback and be comfortable doing so whenever it is needed.

One of the most important tasks that a coach will have to accomplish is providing feedback to team members before, during, or after a coaching event. We started this section of the book with a scenario in which the manager was providing feedback to his team member about his performance. We also discussed that feedback typically opens the door to coaching, but it can also occur as part of a coaching event and can be used as a follow-up after one as well as throughout the entire coaching relationship.

We discussed earlier that people typically conflate feedback and coaching; both are usually perceived as delivering negative information. The fact is, as a coach, you should think of both as positive actions that are taken at all times, in planned and unplanned circumstances, to help your team member to grow professionally and personally. A coach should give coaching and feedback to team members to positively influence and guide behaviors, so that they can excel by improving performance or accomplishing a goal.

Two types of feedback can achieve these results. The first is redirecting feedback. Provide redirecting feedback when you want to guide your team member in another direction. For example, if the decision that the team member has made will result in a less than desirable outcome, you may want the team member to consider other options or make another choice. The second type of feedback is called reinforcing feedback. An effective coach finds opportunities to provide reinforcing feedback by encouraging and praising team members when they accomplish performance, professional or personal goals or are making progress towards accomplishing them.

COMPONENTS OF EFFECTIVE FEEDBACK

How do you provide feedback during a coaching relationship?

Well, it must first be understood that good feedback needs to contain certain elements; it must *be balanced, specific, timely, behavior-based, planned* and *private*. Let's discuss these elements.

When you provide feedback, especially in a coaching relationship, it has to be balanced. What does providing balanced feedback mean?

It means that you are going to identify the positive aspects of an action that the team member has taken, and areas that may need improving. We emphasized earlier that coaching cannot take place in a vacuum, and neither can feedback. To provide good feedback, you will have to create an environment in which feedback is seen as a positive exchange between the coach and the team member, even in the case of redirecting feedback. High levels of trust and strong interpersonal relationships have to be present for both coaching and feedback to be effective. In providing *balanced* feedback, a coach has to know the team member's strengths, talents and accomplishments and use that as a bridge when discussing the area that needs improvement. Discuss what the team member is doing well, then transition to the areas that need more effort. As a coach, you must be *specific* about what your team member is doing well and what needs to improve.

Let's go back to the case of the team member who wants to start a company streaming service. You have put the team member in contact with a decision maker in the marketing department. The marketing team has latched on to the idea and is pleased that this type of talent exists internally. Your team member did not follow up with the marketing contact during an agreed upon time, and the marketing team lead mentioned it to you in passing one day. You will need to provide some feedback to the team member and then open the door to a coaching conversation. To do this, acknowledge the team member for coming up with such a bold idea. Let the team member know how much you and the company value insightful and innovative team members. Ask about the progress made on the idea and with the marketing contact. If the team member has taken responsibility for not following up, some redirecting feedback would be needed to encourage the team member to remain in contact and communicate with the marketing team. Then open the door to coaching.

Let's discuss *timely* and *private* feedback. What does timely mean? Does it mean you have to provide feedback to a team member every time you see an opportunity?

Would you like to receive feedback every time you did something well or every time you did not do something well? Even positive feedback would become annoying or perceived as cloying and insincere if it is done too often. *Timely* feedback means that you will pick the right time and place to provide feedback. In a coaching relationship, allow your team member to self-correct. Remember, the team member knows what to do; sometimes he or she will try things out that might not work and will learn from that experience. Allow the team member to do that.

Now, let's talk about giving feedback in *private*. In a coaching relationship, you will be providing well-timed feedback on an ongoing basis for something a team member has done well or when performance needs improvement. And since coaching usually involves a one-on-one relationship between the coach and the team member, why wouldn't feedback be private, regardless of the type? Well, that might be the case in most coaching relationships. And in all cases, team members should receive private feedback about improving their performance.

But what if you want to recognize a team member for accomplishing a goal and you want to solicit other team members to join you in congratulating or celebrating the team member's accomplishment? Should you forgo the idea of involving others and offer reinforcing feedback under a cloak of secrecy?

There is no right or wrong answer in this instance. It really depends on the desire of the team member you are coaching. That is why it is essential to build that foundation for the coaching relationship. A coach must have insight into the preferences of each team member. It never hurts to ask the team member for guidance. It may be that the team member wants to be private in one situation and may relish in the publicity in another.

Planning feedback is necessary because it allows you to reflect on the team member as a person with goals, values and challenges, both on and off the job. You can think about the overall performance of the team member so that you can deliver balanced feedback. Another reason to plan is that it allows you to do your homework so that you can provide information that is *specific* to the situation to which the feedback is being provided. Winging it can have disastrous consequences!

During an actual coaching conversation, you will likely unearth new information that will require feedback, and you will not have the time to plan it.

What do you do in that case?

Well, you might not be able to plan the feedback while you are engaged in a coaching conversation, but you can plan before you enter a coaching session. Remember, as a coach, you are influencing and guiding your team members. Your team members have the answers, and you are challenging and influencing them through listening and asking valuable questions to help them get to where they need to be. With that in mind, you should know that you are like a driving instructor, who is in the passenger seat guiding the team member. You should have a plan ahead of time about what you want to focus on and the outcome you are expecting, so planning is always essential when providing feedback, regardless of when the feedback occurs.

Let's discuss being specific when you provide feedback.

Being *specific* helps the team member to understand your perspective as a coach and the behavior that needs reinforcing or redirecting. In the case of the team member who is not following up with the marketing department, you will need specific information. Find out from the team member or the marketing contact when the follow-up was requested and what took place that prevented the meeting from happening. You also need to be able to identify the behavior that you want the team member to change. On the surface, it might seem as if the team member forgot to follow up or has lost interest, but the behavior may be based on something else. Get to the root of why the behavior is occurring and discuss what needs to change. As discussed earlier, communication should be non-judgmental; present your feedback in a neutral manner. This will help to reassure your team member that you have no hidden agenda, except to influence that person to improve performance or accomplish a goal.

GOAL TYPES

And speaking of goals, feedback, like coaching, cannot be given without any grounding. When you provide feedback, it should be linked to something that is to be achieved; its results can be measured or is objectively observable and based on some standard. Your feedback should be based on a performance, professional development or personal goal.

Let's discuss the three goal types.

A performance goal is usually job-related with the intent to improve one's performance in a technical, behavioral aspect of the job, or both. For example, the goal may be to complete 50 sales orders in one hour within the next two weeks, an improvement over the team member's current 45 sales orders per hour. The team member will need to decide how to come up with a plan to meet the goal. That plan is usually presented in the form of objectives.

Objectives are specific steps that will be taken towards accomplishing a goal. As part of meeting that goal, the team member may learn that more collaboration is needed with other team members; this is now a behavioral goal that has to be accomplished to meet the overarching technical goal of completing 50 sales orders in one hour within the next two weeks.

Behavioral goals are sometimes harder to measure or quantify. So, the team member will need to reflect on current collaboration levels, identify ways to collaborate more in order to meet the target, and then come up with a specific plan or objective to achieve this goal.

Now, sometimes a team member's professional development goal will be broader in scope. The team member may aspire to serve in a management role inside or outside of your department or the company. Certain trainings or certifications may be required to increase the team members' value to the organization and or earning potential.

Other team members may have goals that are not directly related to the job. For example, a personal goal to travel or learn a foreign language. Should a coach be concerned with a team member's personal goal?

Coaching is about improving performance of the team member and ultimately, the organization. So can the personal goal, learning a foreign language, benefit the organization?

Indeed it can. Your team members, like you, are complex beings with professional and personal needs that are often intertwined. You cannot extricate the professional side of the person and leave the other parts untouched. The best coaches learn to support the whole person, which in turn builds trust and maintains strong interpersonal relationships with team members. And we know that trust forms the basis for effective coaching relationships. When you focus on the whole person, team members will realize that you are interested in them and not just what you can get from them. This increases job satisfaction. Satisfied employees are engaged and produce more than dissatisfied employees. So, the organization does benefit from coaches who focus on the personal and professional needs, desires, and goals of the whole person.

The elements of good feedback discussed so far, then, help team members perform better when it is related to performance, professional or personal goals. Feedback during a coaching relationship should be ongoing and should be given when things are going well, not going well, or going as expected. Feedback that is anchored to a goal helps team members and the coach to focus on what is to be accomplished and how it will be accomplished and shows when it is accomplished. When team members know what is expected of them, then the goal-related feedback helps clarify those expectations to ensure that goals are met.

Remember, effective feedback should be planned, specific, behavior-based, balanced, timely, and private, if necessary. The feedback that you give as a coach will be either redirecting or reinforcing. When the objective is to have someone stop, change, or modify a behavior, redirecting feedback is given to have someone continue demonstrating a behavior, reinforcing feedback is appropriate.

In a coaching relationship in which the team member knows how to accomplish a goal, has the motivation but lacks confidence, and you are tapped to be the coach, which type of feedback would you expect to give more frequently to this person?

As the saying goes, *encouragement sweetens labor*; certainly, you should expect to give reinforcing feedback.

BEING A SOUNDING BOARD

At the end of the day, when you enter into a coaching relationship with your team member, what the team member needs from you more than anything is to be a good *sounding board*. A sounding board is a person who is trusted, a proven listener, and a giver of non-judgmental and non-leading feedback. While not always the case, a sounding board has experience that can be leveraged to validate or enrich the ideas of team members who seek a safe space to verbalize and test these ideas.

Have you ever been approached by someone who just wants to think out loud with you?

Chances are you played the role of sounding board to that person. A sounding board does not exist to dole out answers and advice; the primary duty of a sounding board is to listen and ask carefully crafted, non-biased questions that will stimulate creative thoughts.

COACHING COMMUNICATIONS

Now that you understand the coaching behaviors that are associated with the *Communicate* element, it's time to focus on the mechanics of communicating in a coaching relationship.

How do you actually begin a coaching relationship?

As a leader, you should communicate, gather information and seek opportunities daily to coach your team. Be available for them to engage you. Constantly seek to identify their needs and know when one of those needs is coaching. A major part of being effective in your role is to be able to diagnose team members' needs. A misdiagnosis could be a sign that you have not fostered the right level interpersonal relationship with your team members.

So, how do you identify a coaching need?

It's often the case, as discussed earlier, that the coaching need may present itself when your team member requests coaching, typically when that person knows how to do the job but lacks confidence. It may not be immediately evident to you or the team member that you are about to enter into a coaching conversation, which may blossom into a coaching relationship over an identified goal. As a great communicator, you will ask questions, clarify and confirm information, and use the knowledge you've gained to take the team member to the desired destination.

What if during the course of gathering information, you determined that the team member has the knowledge to perform a task or accomplish a goal but is not motivated to do so? Would you offer coaching to the team member?

Well, can you think of personal tasks or resolutions you have made but did not follow through on them because you were not motivated or just lacked the discipline? Popular goals that people have set are to eat healthier, lose weight, get more education, have more work/life balance, or save more for retirement. A work-specific goal could be to become more adept at the less desirable part of your job. Could a coach help you accomplish those goals?

The answer is—it depends on the person.

Some people can and do accomplish goals, even if they are not motivated at first. They see some value in accomplishing the goals and, over time, they will gain the motivation needed to achieve them. Other people may not have the motivation and are comfortable with the status quo, although accomplishing the goal would be nice.

Have you ever heard people constantly complain about the way something is, but they never make an effort to improve the issue? Yes, some people seem to get therapeutic advantages from speaking out about a desired state without putting forth the effort themselves to get to that desired state.

As we've emphasized, it is critical to build the right kind of interpersonal relationships with your team members. Doing so enables you to give them the support they need, even if that means providing redirecting feedback.

Yes, for team members who know how to perform a job or task and are not performing because they lack the motivation, redirective feedback may be needed, followed by an open door to coaching. Possible coaching outcomes in this case could be refocusing their skills and talents in another role inside or outside the team or outside the company. Since there can be unintended outcomes when one coaches, it is essential for the coach and team member to be clear about the purpose of the coaching relationship, what will be the expected outcome, and what roles the coach and team member will play.

As discussed, there is no script in coaching. Everyone's situation will be different. You will have to employ critical thinking skills to help your team members get to where they want to go. As also discussed, honesty is important to building trust. However, honesty without regard for the self-esteem of the team member you are coaching will also defray trust. Brutal honesty will not work well for some team members. That is why knowing the preferences of team members before introducing a coaching relationship is highly recommended.

Being aware of your physical coaching environment is also important. You cannot coach in a busy, noisy environment or when you are distracted. Create a coaching environment that is distraction free and allows the team member to speak freely without fear of being overheard or somewhat exposed. You may be coaching geographically dispersed or virtual team members and do not have the luxury of physical face-to-face interaction. The coaching experience between virtual and local team members should not be different except that communications with virtual team members will occur using telecommunication devices like telephones, or video conferencing software like Skype or GoToMeeting. In the same way, culturally diverse team members should feel comfortable speaking freely with you as a coach because you understand and respect them as team members and they you, as a coach.

Emphasized frequently in this section of the book is the use of strong interpersonal skills as the key ingredient in a successful coaching relationship. However, to build interpersonal relationships, the coach has to be self-aware. We will discuss more about this when we examine the *Open* element.

Given the time spent examining the *Communicate* element of the COACH framework, you might be reflecting on accidental coaching sessions you've had and missed coaching opportunities. So let's focus on your communication as a coach.

How different is your communication as a coach than regular day-to-day communication? Every opportunity to communicate is an equal opportunity to listen attentively and ask questions to guide your team member's decisions. In a coaching relationship, listening to and understanding others' perspective is essential, so your communication skills need to be polished before you can engage in a meaningful coaching relationship.

Every one of your team members comes to the job with certain values and beliefs about everything. You also possess your own values and beliefs, which may sometimes not align with members on your team. So how does a leader effectively coach a team member with different or contrasting values and beliefs?

As discussed earlier, as a coach, the focus should not be on yourself; it is about you helping team members achieve their aspirations.

Let's return to the Jamie scenario we started earlier. Jamie's manager, Paul, is meeting with him to discuss the performance problem.

Paul: Jamie, I noticed that the error rates have increased on your shift and many of those errors are coming from your area. We sent some help to your area, but the errors are continuing. Tell me what's happening.

Jamie: I know why the error rates are high. I would have explained it to you if I knew that you were going to assign other people to do my job.

Communicate

Paul: I am sorry; I didn't give you an opportunity to explain the situation earlier. Help me understand what the problem is.

Jamie: No problem, I should have come to you and let you know what was going on, instead of allowing the problem to continue. I have been working with another team member to complete her tasks because she is having a hard time keeping up with her studies in school, and this is her last semester before she graduates. I have been having some challenges keeping up with my schedule and helping her. But I'm her teammate, and I want to help her.

Paul: I am aware that your teammate is in school, and I know the two of you work closely together. I appreciate your working to assist her. You've said that you are having a hard time keeping up with your schedule. We need to keep our targets within reach at all times.

How do you think we can help our team member and still meet our targets?

Jamie: I am usually the first that my teammates call on for help. Maybe I could ask my teammates to ask each other for assistance so that everyone can share the load equally.

Paul: Did I hear you say that you are going to ask your teammate to seek out other capable team members?

Jamie: Yes, why not?

Paul: That's a good idea. What have you learned from this experience?

Jamie: I don't know…that I'm not good at multitasking?

Paul: And I've learned that I need to communicate more frequently with you and learn what's going on in your world. How could you improve professionally from this situation?

Jamie: I could practice being more assertive with team members in order to avoid becoming over extended. I should also improve on how I am managing my time.

Paul: OK, those are appropriate goals. How and when do you plan to accomplish these goals?

Jamie: I am going to start this week. I will keep track of my time this week and come up with ways to help my teammates without sacrificing my time or to respectfully decline offering to directly help my teammates when I don't have the time.

Paul: I like your plan. There are also some courses that you can take to help you manage your time. Anyway, I am always here to bounce around ideas if you want to share your plan for communicating with your peers and get some practice. Just make sure that you seek me out ahead of time.

Jamie: I will take you up on that. I definitely don't mind using you as my guinea pig for these types of things.

In the Jamie scenario, Paul communicated openly by providing *honest feedback* and *encouraged open communication* in order to get to the root of the problem, and opened the door to allow Jamie to identify the problem and come up with solutions to address it. It was obvious from the team member's response that Paul had created an environment of trust that enabled him to approach his team member about the issue. Jamie was able to identify a communication weakness of his boss, who assumed the reason for the poor performance was a lack of resources. There was a lack of resources, but the root cause of the error was that Jamie was over extended. He did not want to say no to his teammates, and he was not managing his time effectively.

In the scenario, Paul openly shares information with Jamie to help him understand the impact his performance has had on the entire team. A coach should keep the lines of communication open at all times between and among team members.

To *help guide the decision of his team member*, Paul asks Jamie to reflect on what he has learned from the experience. An effective coach *withholds judgment, seeks clarity, and gets all the facts before making a decision.* At the very beginning, Paul did not take the time to get the facts before making the decision to assign someone to Jamie's area. This created uneasiness in the relationship between Paul and his team member. Sometimes, when supervisors are coaches, they spend more time managing than leading. They just want to get the task done or solve the problem to maintain the company's desired level of productivity. An effective coach finds opportunities to provide honest feedback and offer coaching to help the team member find the best solution. Despite Paul's blunders at the beginning, his team member still thought of him as a *good sounding board.* The people who work closely with you will be able to evaluate your effectiveness when you lead as a coach, as opposed to managing daily work tasks.

MANAGING AND LEADING

In my book *Leading Made Easy*, I discussed the difference between managing and leading. When you are coaching team members, you are leading. Managing day-to-day operations is one aspect of your role as a leader. However, you provide the greatest value to your team members when you are leading. Coaching requires an investment of time and other resources and is a more intimate way of leading your team member than other forms of leading such as delegating or even training. As with any relationship, the more time and resources that you invest in coaching, the greater the expectation is for substantial dividends. An effective coaching relationship does take time, patience and skills, as outlined in the five elements discussed in this book, but the rewards that the leader and the team member reap from that relationship can be astronomical.

PERSONAL COACHING STORY

Here is a personal story about the rewards of coaching: When I was a department head in Corporate America, I took a personal interest in the success of the members of my department. I would often inquire about their current and future goals and then use the coaching elements to help them achieve those goals. One junior member of the department was a single parent. She poured herself into her two children and did everything that she could to ensure their success—often to the detriment of her own.

One day I asked her, "Who are you going to be in 10 years when your children have moved on to start their own lives?" I didn't intend this question to be a criticism but as a means for her to think about what interests she would pursue when not consumed by the commitments of child rearing. While I considered this to be a simple straightforward question, it caused the team member to become upset requiring some time to regain her composure. Unselfishly, she had not given much thought to her own success but only that of her children.

This simple question turned out to be thought-provoking so that it set in motion her desire to explore and identify her interests, set professional and personal goals, and chart a path to achieve them. We had many conversations over the years that allowed me to use the coaching elements to help her stay the course.

About 10 years after I asked that thought-provoking question, I received a phone call from the former team member. She said, "I want to personally share some good news with you before you saw it on social media." She went on to inform me that she had just received notice that she passed her registered nurse's examination. She had achieved her intermediate goal of becoming a registered nurse and has plans to go on to become a nurse practitioner. It goes without saying that this achievement evoked a feeling of accomplishment for her, but the news also served as a reward for me for coaching her over the years.

Now, to wrap up this discussion on the Communicate element of the COACH framework, it's your turn to reflect on your communication as a coach and how well you display the behaviors in your coaching relationships. You may have unintentionally coached someone and you are now wondering if you did it right. If you modeled the behaviors discussed in the *Communicate* element, chances are you did very well.

Here's an activity for you to take some time to reflect on one or more coaching relationships or discussions you have had. Rate yourself on how well you performed on average, based on the behaviors that are presented in the following table.

SELF-REFLECTION

COMMUNICATE

INSTRUCTIONS

Read each statement below. **Use the 0-5 scale to rate yourself on how often you use the behavior described.** For example, if you demonstrate the behavior most of the time, enter the number four (4) next to that statement. After you've entered all the scores, add them together and place the raw score total in the Raw Score section of the equation and multiply by two (2) to arrive at your total score. Review the explanation that corresponds with your total score, then read the other explanations.

0	1	2	3	4	5
NEVER	RARELY	SOME-TIMES	HALF THE TIME	MOST TIMES	ALWAYS

YOU ꙴ

1.	Communicates effectively.	
2.	Listens attentively to others to help guide their decisions.	

3.	Is perceived by others as a good sounding board.	
4.	Encourages open communication.	
5.	Tries to see things from others' points of view.	
6.	Provides honest feedback.	
7.	Asks for clarity when what is being said is not understood.	
8.	Is an effective listener.	
9.	Rarely makes decisions until he or she has heard all the facts.	
10.	Gives full attention when communicating with others.	
	RAW SCORE ⇨	

	$X2 =$	
RAW SCORE	MULTIPLY BY 2	TOTAL SCORE

79 to 100 (High) — You demonstrate very effective use of the *Communicate element* behaviors. Inspire and help others develop skills to successfully use them.

65 to 78 (Average) — You demonstrate effective use of the *Communicate* element behaviors. Continue working to enhance your ability to use them.

Below 65 (Low) — You demonstrate limited use of the *Communicate* element behaviors. Take advantage of opportunities to enhance your ability to use them.

For a more comprehensive evaluation, the companion COACH[180] assessment is available online. The assessment allows members of your immediate work circle to assess the degree to which you exhibit the behaviors associated with the coaching elements discussed in this book.

Visit **www.AlonzoJohnsonPHD.com** for more information on how to complete the COACH[180] assessment.

OPEN

"Always be open to inspiration. You never know where it may come from. Begin with an open mind, end with an inspired heart."

— Sheri Fink

Think of someone you perceive as open. What makes that person open? Does that person reveal deep, dark secrets to you and perhaps to anyone who would listen? Do you cringe or see other people cringing and making up excuses to be out of that person's presence?

Well, that person does not exemplify the behaviors in the Open element of the COACH framework. Coaches who are open *seek to develop relationships with others*, then *build and maintain those relationships* over time or within a certain span of time. The best coaches *relate well with others because they are adept at reading the emotional state of others*. They *are empathetic in their dealings with others and, as a result, are aware of the needs and feelings of others*. Effective coaches are also *approachable and make others feel comfortable discussing issues or speaking their minds because they don't judge others for what they say or do*.

So, if the duty of a coach is to take team members to their desired professional or personal destinations, why does the coach need to demonstrate these behaviors? Won't the team member arrive at the destination if the coach communicates well, ensures that the team member is in alignment with the goal, collaborates with that team member to get there, and in the process, harnesses the team member's untapped ability?

In a nutshell, the answer is, yes. You can coach team members successfully by demonstrating the behaviors outlined in the other elements of the COACH framework. But being successful isn't the same as being effective. Answer these questions: Have you ever been on a bus, in a taxi, Uber or Lyft ride and you want to get information from the driver about an unfamiliar destination, but the driver did not interact with you the way you needed? Did you have to load your bag into the car and unload it when you arrived at your destination? The driver did not even tell you when you even arrived. Even if you have never experienced this treatment firsthand, being as empathetic as you are, how would you feel after you arrived at your destination? How would you feel about the driver and the overall travel experience? Chances are the experience took away from the excitement of your trip. And if you were asked to provide a review of the driver and experience, it would likely not be so positive, and neither would the tip! The driver got to the destination successfully but was not effective in creating a pleasant travel experience.

An effective coach creates engaging and satisfying experiences for team members, while guiding them to accomplish their desired goals successfully. Let's spend some time exploring why effective coaches demonstrate behaviors that are consistent with the Open element of the COACH framework.

BUILDING AND MAINTAINING RELATIONSHIPS

In the *Communicate* section, trust is discussed as the bedrock of effective coaching relationships. Coaches have to be open with their team members to build trusting relationships. An effective coach *seeks to develop, build and maintain relationships with others.*

You might think the team member who needs coaching should initiate and build the relationship. That is true to an extent. You want to empower your team members to seek out the right relationships to help them get to where they want to go. Those relationships may or may not be with you or anyone else on your team. However, as an effective coach, your duty is to lay the groundwork for effective and mutually beneficial coaching relationships and outcomes. Part of seeking to develop relationships is to communicate effectively, listen attentively, and observe your team members in order to learn about them and what makes them unique. You cannot learn if you do not create the right environment.

Think about the most meaningful relationship that you've built and fostered over the years. What did you do during the budding years of that relationship? Did you begin in a way that let the person know that you were interested in a relationship? Then after you established rapport, did you reveal something about yourself to the person?

Why did you do that?

You did that because you know that if you revealed something about yourself, the other person, if interested in a relationship, would reciprocate. You also did that because at that point, you were searching for common ground. It is much easier to build a relationship when there are commonalities among the coach and team members.

Does this mean that a coaching relationship will suffer if the coach and the team member have very little, if anything, in common?

Well, do not be too quick to conclude that commonalities do not exist. We are complex beings, but common threads connect us, even though we may not look or sound the same. An effective coach will take the time to explore commonalities at the beginning and throughout the relationship. Developing and building relationships based on commonalities is a natural approach for human beings. Human beings learn by connecting like pieces of information and then making sense of them.

As discussed in the *Communicate* section, the brain has mental models or filing cabinets for all of the information it gathers using the five senses. When new information comes in, the brain searches for a cabinet with like information and files it away there.

While the human brain is wired to connect the known with the unknown, developing, building, and maintaining relationships isn't always about finding commonalities. An effective coach should not just be open to learning about team members but also learning from them. Although coaching is focused on accomplishing goals, the coach has to meet team members where they are—on their grounds. Sometimes, it requires coaches to step away from their own mental models and explore areas that are unfamiliar or even uncomfortable. Showing genuine interest in the team member being coached goes a long way to gaining respect and trust.

BEING GENUINE

The word *genuine* is important, especially in coaching. People can decipher relationship-building attempts that are only a means to an end. These attempts are commonly known as "checking the box." Developing and building relationships to help team members accomplish a goal doesn't come by just checking the box.

Have you ever been to a restaurant and your order did not come out right and the server asks about your experience? You explain the issue and the server retorts, "I'm sorry," but does nothing to address the issue? How sorry do you think the server feels about what happened?

Saying "I'm sorry" is a learned behavior; wait staff are trained to check in on customers and apologize if the goods or services don't meet their expectations—that is an example of checking the box. Fixing the problem would be a much more convincing task.

In a coaching relationship, the coach has to be tuned into the team member being coached. If you are not totally invested or not interested in coaching that person, it will show in your body language. Your lack of interest could be caused by something that is not related to the act of coaching. It could be that you are not fond of the person's personality or mannerism, or you may not be enthusiastic about the goal or topic that the team member wants to explore.

As a leader, it is your duty to coach. There are always parts of your job that you might not find enjoyable, and coaching may very well be one of them. But you have accepted the role—to lead all of your team members. The organization and your team members expect you to manage and lead your team effectively; coaching those who need it is one of, if not the best way to show leadership. Remember, while you may grow professionally or otherwise from a coaching relationship, you are not center stage in the coaching relationship. Regardless of the coaching situation, an effective coach must be willing and able to lead by navigating the way for all team members and all others who are supporting them throughout the process.

RELATIONSHIP MOTIVATORS

As discussed earlier in the *Communicate* section, a coaching relationship requires an investment of time on the part of the coach and the team member. As a result, these relationships run the risk of becoming stale, especially when the goal is not achievable within a short timeframe or several objectives must be mastered before the goal is achieved. Motivation may wane for the coach and team member. Building the relationship is a great start; maintaining its momentum requires a more deliberate effort.

So, how does a coach build and maintain relationships that will keep team members motivated along the coaching journey?

Well, trust is one of the biggest motivators in any relationship. One of the tools that you can use to build and maintain open and trusting coaching relationships is the Johari Window, a tool developed by psychologists in 1955. When the tool is used correctly, it opens windows to our being and allows us to gain valuable insights about ourselves from a variety of perspectives.

The Johari Window presents four perspectives or panes, drawn from the way we view ourselves and how we are perceived by others.

Pane 1: Parts that we see and others see **Open**	Pane 2: Parts that we are not aware of that others see **Blind Spot**
Pane 3: Parts that we know but keep from others **Hidden**	Pane 4: The unconscious or subconscious parts that are not seen by us or others **Unknown**

The first pane, the Open Area, displays parts that we are aware of, accept, and are comfortable with others seeing. Pane 2, the Blind Spot, reveals parts that other people see but are not part of our awareness. Pane 3 is called the Hidden Area because these are the parts that we know but keep from others. Pane 4, the Unknown Area, reveals parts that are not known to us and not seen by others. This area contains our greatest potential for growth personally and professionally.

The purpose of the Johari Window tool is to expand the Open pane of both the coach and the team member. You can use the Johari Window as an activity at the beginning or at any point during the coaching experience to provide a greater context on which to build a strong coaching relationship. Along with fostering trust, exploring the Johari Window during a coaching relationship encourages greater levels of collaboration and enhances self-awareness.

SELF-AWARENESS

Being aware of self is foundational to developing any type of meaningful relationship; a coaching relationship is no exception. The Johari Window helps the coach and the team member to become more aware of themselves and each other. As a coach, you will discover more about yourself and become more self-aware by listening to feedback from others about your blind spots; we all have them.

During the course of the coaching relationship, you might come to a point when you will reveal things about yourself that are not known by most people who know you, and the team member who is being coached might share little known personal information, too. Do not judge the team member for holding certain views or making decisions that you don't understand or would not recommend.

Self-examination is a necessary component of being self-aware and a required task for a coach. Coaches must examine themselves frequently and root out any hidden biases or prejudices that they may harbor. In order to motivate team members to accomplish a goal, a coach has to instill confidence in their ability to accomplish the goal while also acknowledging that mistakes are part of the process. Even the best coaches will make mistakes. As a coach, you are also a leader. Take stock of your actions and freely admit flaws; learn from them and leverage your strengths. This will encourage your team member to feel comfortable viewing mistakes as learning opportunities.

Earlier, in the *Communicate* section we examined non-judgmental and non-leading communication. In the instance when a team member shares information with you that may be private or of a sensitive nature, the natural impulse is to put up a personal measuring tape against that information and make a judgment based on your mental models. A good coach remains neutral and open to multiple perspectives.

For a team member to share information that is hidden from general consumption requires a high level of trust. A coach should never sabotage that trust by inserting opinions that are only based on a limited frame of reference or mental models. Listen with an open mind, ask questions and understand the perspective from which the team member is communicating. There may be cultural, gender, ethnic and other perspectives or a combination of perspectives from which the team member is communicating. Your duty as a coach is to seek understanding so that you can help get that team member to the desired professional or personal destination. By withholding judgment, you will be seen as someone who is highly approachable and unbiased.

BEING APPROACHABLE

A coach should not be unreachable to team members from a physical, mental, emotional, and spiritual standpoint. During every coaching encounter, team members should feel comfortable discussing any issue with their coach or speaking up about any issue that is of concern. A coach should be *approachable and make others feel comfortable discussing issues or speaking their minds*, regardless of the political correctness of the topic.

As a coach, you are already in a position of power because the team member you are coaching either reports to you or is removed from you based on hierarchical structure. This power can be a barrier to team members fully expressing their views about pertinent topics. So it is essential to find ways to neutralize that power distance during the relationship, while still preserving it. Certainly, being open about your strengths and shortcomings, fears and hopes for the future is one way of opening the door to yourself and allowing the team member to see you as a human being first, rather than a boss.

SHARING RESPONSIBLY

Just remember, the more open the pane is in your Johari Window, the more likely team members will be at ease in opening up to you. This in no way means that you are to share information about yourself that has no bearing on the coaching relationship and that you are uncomfortable sharing. Do not share information that you do not wish to hear repeated by anyone. That is not to say you are not to trust the team member you are coaching, but you should remember that once the words leave your lips, they cannot be withdrawn. So be discerning of the information you share to build rapport and trust during a coaching relationship. As I always say, "share but share responsibly."

Are you wondering about just how much you can share as an Open coach?

It really depends on your level of openness and that of the team member you're coaching. Some team members require more time to get to know you as a coach, while others will want to dive into the relationship and get to action planning to accomplish the goal. Some people are very open and expect that people will be open with them and when that does not happen they may withdraw or modify their behavior during the relationship.

A tool that can help gauge a person's level of openness is the FIRO Element B™ (Fundamental Interpersonal Relationship Orientation-Element Behavior™). This tool measures yours and your team member's level of openness, inclusiveness and control within the context of what one needs, what one gets, and how satisfied one is with the results. You can use this tool as a general team-building tool or use it during a one-on-one coaching relationship with each of your team members. The tool may reveal discrepancies between what you or the team members expect of each other and what you actually get, providing an avenue for further exploration and discoveries.

So, tools such as the FIRO Element B™ and the Johari Window can be used to gain insights into the inherent characteristics or preferences of team members. These insights can be used to build and maintain interpersonal relationships with those you coach.

CONNECTING EMOTIONALLY

Effective coaches should know their team members enough to become *adept at reading their emotional state as well as their needs and feelings*. The ability to read the emotional state of another human being is called empathy—the ability to place oneself in another person's position and experience how that person feels and understands what needs to be satisfied. You cannot develop this skill overnight. It comes from building relationships and through gathering information using your senses—these are the windows to your brain that will process the information. You have to tap into the verbal and non-verbal behaviors of the team member you are coaching. You should be able to tell when the team member is frustrated, happy or sad—just a few from a range of human emotions. Be consistent in the way that you take time to learn about them and how you respond to their needs and feelings. Your team members will make decisions about you and who you are based on the behaviors that you display.

Let's put this statement in concrete terms: A coach or leader who has empathy has the ability to listen attentively and is well-equipped to read the emotional state of others and react appropriately to each team member. As we discussed in the *Communicate* and in this section, you will listen not only to one's words but observe the body language that accompanies those words. Is the person exhibiting positive or negative emotions? Examine the facial expressions during conversations. This will help you to understand the true feelings behind the spoken words. For example, does the person's smile look sincere? Remember, how a person feels is often visible on the face, but this is not always the case. Take into account the individual's cultural background because people sometimes express emotions based on their culture or upbringing.

EMOTIONAL INTELLIGENCE

Most importantly, as a coach, you need a high level of emotional intelligence to read the emotional state and gain insight into the needs and feelings of your team member.

Let's spend some time discussing the term, emotional intelligence. When we hear the word intelligence, most of us immediately associate it with someone who is mentally smart with a high IQ, and we are not wrong. Another form of intelligence, emotional intelligence, is equally or perhaps more important, especially for people who find themselves in leadership positions and have to execute the art of coaching. Emotional intelligence allows leaders to recognize and navigate the emotions of self and others. It is a powerful tool for leaders when it is harnessed and used effectively, especially in a coaching situation.

Emotional and social skills are critical in leadership. These skills determine how we perceive and express ourselves, as well as how we perceive others and maintain relationships with them. Being an emotionally intelligent leader means that you are aware of your emotions and that of your team members. Coaching can be an emotional journey and your success or failure as a coach is dependent on how well you demonstrate that you are aware of your emotional cues and those of the team member you are coaching.

Here are some examples of behaviors of those who possess both low and high emotional intelligence. Examples of low emotional intelligent behavior include not being able to take constructive or redirective feedback, laying blame on others, making passive-aggressive comments, giving opinions that are not relevant or valuable, and playing the victim when there may not be one at all. Coaches with low emotional intelligence may not listen to the recommendations of team members on how to accomplish a goal and may be out of touch with those they lead.

Coaches and team members who possess high levels of emotional intelligence are much more self-aware. In the workplace, this translates to a coach and a team member who understand their strengths and weaknesses and how their actions affect other team members and the organization. In other words, high levels of emotional intelligence result in self-aware coaches and team members who are better equipped to receive and handle redirective feedback and learn from their mistakes.

Coaches or team members with high emotional intelligence control their own emotions and exercise restraint when required—they demonstrate the ability to self-regulate. Emotionally intelligent people are also self-motivated, not so much by money and title but also by a greater internal ambition and drive; this is known as intrinsic motivation. When they encounter disappointment, they possess the ability to remain optimistic and resilient. A coach with high emotional intelligence will genuinely respond to a team member's concerns and build rapport and trust quickly and effectively.

Do you think a leader with low emotional intelligence can be effective as a coach?

Of course not.

Any person who steps into the role of coach must possess a high degree of emotional intelligence to be effective. Coaching is not a check-the-box exercise; the purpose of a coaching relationship is to transform the team member who is being coached. An emotionally intelligent coach listens to the thoughts that are expressed by team members in a manner that shows them that they are important to the success and growth of the organization and their professional and personal growth is a priority. Show all team members that you value them as persons through your actions by demonstrating empathy.

BEING EMPATHETIC

You cannot fake being empathetic. If the emotion is not genuine, it will show. Earlier in this section, we discussed the importance of being reachable physically, emotionally and spiritually to your team member. One of the sure-fire ways to show your lack of commitment to the coaching relationship and lack of empathy is through your nonverbal behaviors. When in a coaching relationship, be present. You can't give your full attention if you are secretly trying to keep up with the score of your favorite sports team, glancing at text messages, or you are wondering what you will eat for lunch or dinner. As stated in the *Communicate* section, if you are not able to give the team member your undivided attention, put off the conversation until you have the time. One bad meeting could cause irreparable damage to a coaching relationship.

Putting empathy to use helps identify the problem and help find a solution or, at least, find a way to help guide the team member through the problem. Showing your team members that you understand, care about them, and are willing to help them find solutions when they have problems will enhance your skills as a coach and help you gain the respect of your team members. They will know that you truly care about them and not just about their contribution to the organization.

A part of relating well and being empathetic with your team members is validating or acknowledging their beliefs. We are already aware that you and your team member may not always share the same beliefs. As a result, you will make decisions or act in ways that might not be aligned with each other's beliefs. Demonstrating in words and deeds that you understand the person's perspective goes a long way towards building trusting coaching relationships. Remember, validating and agreeing are two different things. Sometimes, all your team members need is to get their feelings out, and an open coach, through non-judgmental listening, can demonstrate that he or she understands how the person feels. This alone will often positively influence the team member to open up and, in so doing, strengthen the bond of a great coaching relationship.

To summarize this *Open* section, a coach must consistently demonstrate honesty, emotional intelligence and empathy to move the team member toward accomplishing established goals. In a trusting environment, both the coach and the team member feel comfortable sharing ideas, providing honest feedback, and challenging the status quo to stir critical thinking to accomplish goals.

To maintain constructive relationships, both the coach and the team member must be willing to show respect for each other and remain open to receiving and giving constructive feedback. To do this, it is essential for the coach to listen effectively and ask questions to clarify information. To ensure that you are building and maintaining a constructive relationship, ensure that your verbal and nonverbal cues are aligned. You also need to be self-aware and remain objective because your values can color the message you send.

Put yourself in the shoes of the team member and try to gain understanding from that perspective, then use critical thinking skills to analyze the information that you receive. Finally, use that information to influence and challenge the team member to find the best path forward.

Now that you're familiar with the behaviors associated with the Open element of the COACH framework, let's see how the use of the Open elements would appear in a coaching event. Keep an eye out for behaviors associated with the Communicate element, too. Read the scenario below and see if you can identify behaviors that are consistent with the *Open* element.

SCENARIO

Background: Marcy has been a team leader for seven years. She values her team members and finds ways to help them succeed on the job. Jan, one of her team members, is meeting with her to discuss advancement opportunities.

Jan: Hi Marcy. May I speak with you for a few minutes?

Marcy: Sure, I have some time right now. What's going on?

Jan: I have been in this role for the past five years and I've been thinking about spreading my wings.

Marcy: That's good to hear! Tell me more about what you are thinking.

Jan: I recently completed a degree in marketing, and I'm ready to put that degree to work.

Marcy: Good! I am glad you are thinking about improving yourself professionally. I really admire team members who seek out opportunities to grow professionally. You have definitely done well in your role. I've delegated a number of tasks to you over the years; you are a quick learner, so I do understand your desire to do more. Marketing is significantly different from your area. I want to support your professional growth, even if it's not within my department. How do you plan to make the transition?

Jan: I understand that I don't have any marketing experience, so I am willing to take an entry-level position. I know it sounds crazy, but I've gotten bored with my position, and there is nowhere to grow in the department, so I'd like to try something different.

Marcy: I understand how you must feel. I've been there. It must be uneasy even considering moving from a senior position to an entry-level position.

Jan: Yes, the salary difference will be significant, and I'm a little nervous.

Marcy: Have you thought about how you will bridge the salary gap while transitioning?

Jan: Well, not really. I don't have all the answers yet, but I have applied for a position in the marketing department.

Marcy: I see the position is open to internal and external candidates. How do you plan to stand out as a candidate?

Jan: Maybe I can speak with someone in that department about the job and the skills and personality that they are looking for. I planned to ask you to put in a good word for me.

Marcy: Sure thing! I'd be happy to speak with the hiring manager. I know this is a big step for you. What else would you like me to do to support you?

In the scenario, it is clear that Marcy took the time to develop relationships with her team members, and she was able to build and maintain those relationships. A team member would not divulge job-hunting information to a manager, if the environment of trust were not created. Jan also expressed that she is not challenged in the department. Some managers would view that as a sign of weakness on their part—not Marcy.

Marcy was able to relate to Jan's feeling of boredom with the role and could empathize with the emotions that Jan was feeling just by considering such a drastic move. Additionally, Marcy knew that Jan was at the top of the pay grade in her unit and seemed to have been expecting her to look for other opportunities. The discussion was very power-neutral because Marcy made a decision not to judge Jan's decision to seek a second career.

PERSONAL STORY

I'd like to share a personal example of a coaching relationship that required me to be open. During my tenure in the U.S. Army, I had the privilege of serving as a senior leader of a Basic Training Company. Basic training is known to many as boot camp. I realize that most people don't think of army leaders as being open—especially within the context of basic training or boot camp, but the need to be open often presents itself during some of the most stressful times in our lives.

One day while inspecting the physical fitness training for each platoon, I noticed that one of the platoons was without a drill sergeant. When I inquired about the whereabouts of the drill sergeant, the young trainees of the platoon informed me that he was in the barracks having a discussion with a member of the platoon—a trainee who wanted to quit basic training.

I went to the barracks where the drill sergeant and trainee were having the discussion to offer my help. After observing the discussion for a moment, I noticed that it was very intense and the young trainee wanted only one thing—to be discharged from the Army. I informed the drill sergeant that I would take over the discussion with the young man so the drill sergeant could resume physical fitness training with his platoon.

After talking with the trainee for a short while, I realized that the reason he wanted to quit basic training was that he felt alone. He thought that no one understood the anxieties that he was experiencing from participating in basic training. I began sharing stories about basic training anxieties that I experienced when I was a young trainee. I informed him that these anxieties were quite normal—a lot of trainees have them during basic training, although they may not share them. I shared with him that basic training was so mentally taxing for me that I would sometimes cry at nights in bed. I walked him through some positive self-affirmations that he could practice several times a day.

The result of my open talk with that young man was nothing short of remarkable. The trainee became so motivated that I would often seek him out to talk to other trainees who had lost motivation and wanted to quit basic training. And he was always happy to help.

Now it's your turn to reflect on your level of openness as a coach and how well you display Open behaviors in your coaching relationships.

Take some time to reflect on one or more coaching relationships or discussions you have had. Rate yourself on how well you performed on average, based on the behaviors that are presented on the following page.

SELF-REFLECTION

OPEN

INSTRUCTIONS

Read each statement below. Use the 0-5 scale to rate yourself on how often you use the behavior described. For example, if you demonstrate the behavior most of the time, enter the number four (4) next to that statement. After you've entered all the scores, add them together and place the raw score total in the Raw Score section of the equation and multiply by two (2) to arrive at your total score. Review the explanation that corresponds with your total score, then read the other explanations.

0	1	2	3	4	5
NEVER	RARELY	SOME-TIMES	HALF THE TIME	MOST TIMES	ALWAYS

YOU ∪

11.	Is empathetic in dealings with others.	
12.	Relates well with others.	

13.	Builds and maintains constructive relationships.	
14.	Seeks to develop relationships with others.	
15.	Is aware of the needs and feelings of others.	
16.	Is adept at reading the emotional state of others.	
17.	Is approachable and puts others at ease.	
18.	Makes others feel comfortable discussing issues.	
19.	Allows others to speak their minds.	
20.	Doesn't judge others for what they say.	
	RAW SCORE ⮕	

RAW SCORE	MULTIPLY BY 2	TOTAL SCORE
	X2 =	

79 to 100 (High) — You demonstrate very effective use of the *Open* element behaviors. Inspire and help others develop skills to successfully use them.

65 to 78 (Average) — You demonstrate effective use of the *Open* element behaviors. Continue working to enhance your ability to use them.

Below 65 (Low) — You demonstrate limited use of the *Open* element behaviors. Take advantage of opportunities to enhance your ability to use them.

For a more comprehensive evaluation, the companion COACH[180] assessment is available online. The assessment allows members of your immediate work circle to assess the degree to which you exhibit the behaviors associated with the coaching elements discussed in this book.

Visit **www.AlonzoJohnsonPHD.com** for additional information on how to complete the COACH[180] assessment

ALIGN

*"If you align expectations with reality,
you will never be disappointed."*

— Terrell Owens

What images come to mind when you see or hear the word align? Do objects or people presented in a uniformed or orderly manner come to mind?

How often do you hear the phrase, "we're on the same page or on the same sheet of music" or "the stars must be aligned" when something goes well? To align is usually viewed as a positive action that takes place in everyday life. Think about aligning your vehicle or going to the dentist to have alignment work done. Sometimes the process may be costly or uncomfortable, but the results make it worthwhile.

Alignment in coaching happens the way it is perceived in everyday life. In a coaching environment, the coach and the team member being coached have to develop line of sight between where that team member is and where that person wants to go. A coach has to be concerned about the goals that are to be accomplished, the values that the team member possesses and the motivation to accomplish the goals. We will discuss each of these facets within the context of the behaviors associated with the Align element of the COACH framework.

BEING SYSTEMATIC

An effective coach seeks to align with the team member by using a *systematic approach* and incorporate *models* to help accomplish designated goals. Beginning a coaching relationship with the end in mind leads to a more productive and meaningful experience. Therefore, before beginning any coaching relationship, a coach should ask carefully crafted questions, listen attentively and influence the team member to develop the goal and select the most expedient path to accomplish that goal. A systematic approach to coaching allows the coach and the team member to structure the coaching relationship in a manner that supports the accomplishment of the goal. Coaching models are presented as a road map to guide the relationship from the very beginning until the goal(s) is accomplished and may even span beyond goal attainment.

The COACH framework provides a systematic approach for anyone in a coaching role. The framework is focused on effective coaching behaviors that, when practiced, will directly support the team member in achieving the highest level of success in accomplishing targeted goals. Learning the behaviors needed to coach effectively is very important. Having a model to help anchor the coaching relationships provides a consistent and concrete methodology that the coach can apply to each coaching session. The effective coach is able to *use models that will encourage team members to ensure that all goals are accomplished.*

One of the most pragmatic models to use for coaching is GROW. The GROW model is an acronym for **G**oals, **R**eality, **O**ptions, and **W**ill or **W**ay Forward. It is one of the most widely used coaching models to help people who are being coached to clarify what they want to accomplish and determine how to accomplish it. Specifically, this model provides four areas that a coach should explore during a coaching relationship with a team member:

- Setting **G**oals
- Examining Current **R**eality
- Considering **O**ptions
- Determining the **W**ay Forward

Let's spend some time with the GROW model starting with setting goals.

SETTING GOALS

As discussed in the *Communicate* section of this book, goals are used to help team members determine what they want to achieve. These goals may be condensed into more actionable components called objectives. They may also be described as targets, key results, or outcome achievements. Regardless of what they are called, the question to be answered during this phase of the model is "What is the desired result that the team member wants to accomplish?"

Goal-setting in a coaching relationship is like setting your car's GPS to your destination's address. Sometimes given the address you've entered, the GPS will take you to the destination using the most expedient or scenic route. Other times the GPS will not take you to the destination at all because it cannot find the destination.

So what can a coach do to increase the odds that team members will arrive at their desired professional destination in the most expedient or efficient manner possible?

A coach should work with the team member to develop SMART goals or objectives. You probably already know that SMART is an acronym for **S**pecific, **M**easurable, **A**ttainable, **R**elevant and **T**imely. Let's discuss SMART within the context of the *Align* element within the COACH framework.

Align

The goal must be *specific*. There must be a clear understanding of the goal or task, the standard of performance and the expected outcome. In other words, the coach and the team member should know specifically what they are working together to accomplish. For example, if the team member wants a different job in the company, getting that person into the department where the position is gets closer to the goal, but it has not been accomplished—there is still work to be done. The team member might be elated and feels a sense of accomplishment and may not be motivated to engage in the coaching process anymore or may end the coaching relationship prematurely. This is a general example to emphasize that a coach and a team member must be aligned on what exactly is to be accomplished. The details matter.

When goal-setting, some people prefer generalities and are bored by what they consider minutiae. It is essential to point out that goal-setting not only happens at the beginning of the coaching relationship; it can also happen any time throughout the coaching relationship. The team member may have started out specifically wanting a particular position in the department, but may have found that the current job offers more flexibility or more benefits than the one that was previously sought. The team member may have gained confidence during the coaching relationship and wants to have autonomy to accomplish the goal independently after working with the coach to accomplish certain milestones. The coach, therefore, needs to stay vigilant to make sure the goals remain relevant. As established in the *Communicate* section, communication is the glue that connects all the other COACH elements together. An effective coach will be able to align with the team member by listening attentively at all times and asking value-added questions, while maintaining strong interpersonal relationships to gauge whether goals need to be adjusted.

The goal must be *measureable*. How will you and the team member know when the goal or task has been accomplished? If the coach and the team member have done a good job in specifying what must be accomplished, then determining how it will be measured should not be a challenging task. A goal to get a position in another department may seem simple, but it may require a series of other tasks to be accomplished. The team member might need to attend training or get additional schooling to improve technical or soft skills or gain additional experience to be ready for the position. These are tasks, objectives or milestones that have to be satisfied before the ultimate goal can be realized.

The coach and team member, then, must set up success measures for each task to track progress towards the goal. For example, a coaching discussion may involve answers to several questions: how much training or schooling will be needed? What is the level of mastery for the role, and how will it be measured? What soft skills are needed, and how will mastery be measured?

Some goals are more complex than others and will require more sophisticated measurement approaches, like statistical analyses. Coaching is a partnership; work closely with your team members and encourage them to network with others to define standards and tools that are needed to achieve results.

The goal must be something that the team member can achieve. Unreasonable goals can create frustration and possible resentment. For example, setting a goal to complete 100 sales orders in one hour, when the shortest time ever recorded to complete an order is 4 minutes. It would be reasonable for the team member to complete 20 sales orders in an hour. That is not to say that the goals should not challenge your team members to perform at higher than normal levels. We see these challenging goals play out in athletic competitions—one team or athlete strives to outperform the other and set a new record. So in this example, completing 24 sales orders in one hour would probably be a challenging, yet achievable goal for the team member. Challenging goals, sometimes referred to as stretch goals, should provide a motivating and fulfilling experience for the coach and the team member.

So, how do you, as a coach, guide your team member towards choosing challenging, yet achievable goals?

It should come as no surprise that taking time to truly understand your team members is prerequisite for guiding them. Human beings are full of surprises, but as a coach, you should have a very good understanding of the current skillset of the team member and the potential that exists. Some goals require a level effort that may seem daunting at first to the team member, for example, becoming a certified project manager.

You should know the temperament of your team members and whether they have the motivation to persevere and accomplish certain goals. You simply cannot align on setting achievable and challenging goals with someone you don't know; build and maintain those relationships.

Seek to align with your team member on the relevance of the goal. There should be a clear understanding on the part of the coach and team member of how this goal or task fits into the big picture—how does accomplishing this goal benefit the team member and the organization? For example, how would completing 24 sales orders in one hour or becoming a certified project manager achieve either of these ends? A coach must partner with the team member to ensure that the goal, when accomplished, will result in some benefit professionally, personally and organizationally. The latter statement brings back into focus the earlier discussion in the *Communicate* section on whether an organization should always benefit from a coaching relationship.

The answer is, yes.

As we established in the *Communicate* section, coaching is a leadership practice that is employed when a team member knows how to perform a task but lacks the confidence to perform it. The coach, who is dedicating time on the job to coach the team member, should realize some organizational benefits from the relationship. How the benefits are derived may be different, based on the coaching relationship and the goals that are to be accomplished. Coaching for mastery of on-the-job tasks is a clear benefit to the organization because performance improves once the team member masters the task. The team member can train others to perform the task, as an added value to the organization.

Coaching that is geared towards accomplishing a professional goal can also benefit the organization directly. The example of coaching a team member to take on a new position in another department may result in a direct benefit of increased performance, and it can also result in an indirect benefit of greater job satisfaction, which is a catalyst for improved performance. Personal goals, such as traveling and learning about other cultures, are sometimes not related to the job but can offer organizational benefits. Helping the team member realize personal goals will likely cause that team member to view the organization as not just being concerned about its bottom-line but supportive of each person's growth and development. This perception creates a psychological contract between the team member and the organization, which likely will result in a more satisfied and engaged team member. Employees who are satisfied and engaged on the job have longer tenure with the organization.

Every goal that is developed during a coaching relationship must be time-bound; nothing happens in perpetuity; so, each goal should have a specific start and end-point. The goal should be completed within a set timeframe, under certain conditions, or in a certain environment. A savvy coach will review the specific tasks that a team member has to accomplish and then consider the time needed and whether it is reasonable for the team member, based on skill, motivation and resources available. As you would expect, the coach will ask questions, listen attentively, and work with the team member to determine the amount of time that is reasonable to keep the person motivated to attain the goal and measure the outcomes.

Given this discussion of goal-setting within the context of the GROW model, notice that coaches who demonstrate behaviors that are consistent with the Align element do so in partnership with the team member being coached. The coach's role is to assist others in setting development goals that are consistent with their values. The goals that the team member agrees to pursue with guidance from the coach have to align with that person's values and not necessarily with those of the coach. Each section in this book so far has discussed mental models and how the data we gather and our experiences shape those values. In a coaching relationship, a coach has to be mindful of the values that each team member possesses and respectfully navigate the relationship, while being sensitive to those values. The team member who wants to get a position in another department may place a high value on being able to spend quality time with immediate family members. In order to accomplish the goal, the team member may be faced with sacrificing family time in order to complete educational requirements to qualify for the position.

So, what coaching options exist in this case? Should the coach ask the team member to choose between personal values and professional development goals, or should the coach just end the coaching relationship?

Actually, the answer is none of these. A coach should never force team members they are coaching to choose between their values and professional development goals. Neither should the coach give up on team members because there is conflict between what they want and their values. That is why models like GROW are so important to use to structure coaching conversations.

Before formulating a goal, the coach and the team member should examine the realities of what is taking place in each aspect of the team member's life and explore options and the motivation to pursue the goals. Later in this section, we will discuss realities as a component of the GROW model.

An effective coach helps team members set self-improvement goals and then offers advice on how to develop strategies to achieve their career goals. A coaching relationship is only as effective as the goals that are to be accomplished. The discussion on SMART goals pointed out the importance of setting achievable, yet challenging goals. Here, too, as a coach, you will be guiding your team members towards goals that will require them to step out of their comfort zone and exert energy into accomplishing the goal.

And at the beginning of the Open element, we examined the Johari Window to explore blind spots and the window's unknown area. Sometimes, team members are not fully aware of their potential. Your job as a coach is to provide team members with insights into their abilities and encourage them to take calculated risks and unleash untapped potential to improve professionally and personally.

There will also be times when team members set out to accomplish challenging goals but need guidance on how to effectively accomplish them. This is when you can leverage your experience as a leader and coach. While you may have some insight from experience on the strategy that will lead to the team member's success, you want to guide team members in a way that allows them to make decisions and take ownership of the best strategy to undertake to accomplish the goal. Doing so empowers and motivates them to accomplish professional or personal goals that they might not even have thought were possible.

Given this discussion of the goal-setting component of the GROW model within the context of the Align element of the COACH framework, here are possible questions that you can ask to gain alignment on the goals that team members may want to accomplish:

GOALS

- Where do you see yourself in X (number of) years, or months?

- If you had the chance to perform any role, what would that be?

- Now that you have mastered this role/task, have you considered what the next phase will be for you?

- What would you be doing if you were not in this role?

Let's focus on the Reality component of the GROW model.

EXAMINING CURRENT REALITY

When going on a trip, you want to know the road and weather conditions or whether there are toll roads so that you can be prepared to either handle the conditions, detour or delay the trip or find another route or mode of transportation. You're checking the existing reality so you can make the best plans.

What do we mean by reality from a coaching standpoint?

Realities are happenings that are often out of the control of the team member and the coach. They usually have the potential to negatively or positively impact results.

In coaching, if the goal clarifies what the team member is to accomplish, then examining the current realities provides guidance on where to start, what needs to be done and how it must be done. Before settling on the goal, it is important for the coach to work with the team member to develop a detailed understanding of the current realities and how they can support or hinder the accomplishment of set goals.

By identifying current realities, the coach and the team member will avoid building a goal that is based on false assumptions. Let's look again at the example of the team member who aspires to serve in a new position in another department. The reality is that ascending to this position requires sacrifice of the team member's family time. For this person, family time is considered almost sacred.

How should a coach guide the team member in this case?

The coach will encourage the team member to consider current realities before deciding to pursue a goal. In this case, the team member has to accept the reality that in order to advance in his career, some sacrifices will be needed. The team member must decide to pursue the goal with full understanding of the terrain he has to cross to accomplish it.

So how does a coach guide a team member to identify realities?

One of the most common determinants of success or failure to accomplish a goal is the availability of resources. Resources are time, funding, and human capital. It is essential for the coach and the team member to perform frequent reality checks on the resources available to enable that team member to accomplish established goals.

In today's workplace, it is difficult to find time to accomplish anything beyond the normal scope of daily on-the-job tasks. Having the resources to pursue a stretch goal that is not directly linked to daily job performance is typically not a reality for team members. The lack or resouces is a barrier to professional and even personal development.

Organizations typically don't provide funds to support professional development. Oftentimes the team member has to find ways to obtain the necessary funding to pursue these goals. Additionally, gaining access to the right people who can support the team member along the way is often a challenge due to job, family and other types of demands.

Given these realities, a thoughtful coach will direct questions about the resources that are needed and available. Then, allow the team member to refine the goal within the context of the existing reality.

There may be times when the lack of resources alone may not be the reality, but other unforeseen circumstances may loom that threaten achieving the goals. Think about the 2008 Recession. Millions of people were forced to operate in an unstable environment. The stock market plummeted, large banks and part of the automotive industry—GM and Chrysler—went bankrupt. The housing market collapsed and millions of people lost their employment and sizable parts of their pensions. Unforeseen and uncontrollable realities can and do interfere with even the most carefully planned goals. Your team member should develop goals that are flexible enough to be modified.

One of the tools used in marketing is the PESTEL analysis. This tool is used to analyze different contexts: **P**olitical, **E**conomic, **S**ocial, **T**echnological, **E**nvironmental and **L**egal. Although this tool is often used at the macroeconomic level to study large-scale national economic trends, it can be adapted for use in a coaching relationship to review internal and external challenges that may hinder goal attainment. During a coaching session, discuss any political, economic, social, technological, environmental or legal factors that may impede or support goal attainment.

Some goals may not require a full PESTEL analysis, but before deciding on a goal, make sure that the team member knows exactly how things are currently, how they could be in the future and what needs to be done to accomplish the desired goal. Take into consideration all the resources that are needed. Contemplate the challenges, both internal and external to the organization, that might arise and consider how they may be overcome.

Here are examples of questions to ask when examining and trying to bring current reality into clearer focus.

Align

- Will the current *environment* support your efforts?
- Do you have the required skills and knowledge, or will you have to acquire them?
- Where are you now relative to the goal?
- How can you leverage your network to support this goal?
- Whom will you have to involve? What is their availability and willingness to support?
- Do you have the necessary support system and budget?
- What obstacles do you anticipate encountering?

CONSIDERING OPTIONS

The **O** in the GROW model, Options, will provide guidance for how the goal can be accomplished. Reflecting on the road trip analogy used earlier, you need to know alternate routes to get to your destination. Likely, each route has advantages and disadvantages; you have the option of deciding the most advantageous depending on what's important to you. Do you want to get there faster? Do you prefer a more scenic route? Do you mind paying tolls?

In coaching, you and the team member may discuss a goal that needs to be accomplished. You may be aware of some of the factors that can impede goal attainment. Work with the team member to identify all the options that are available to eliminate or minimize those factors to achieve the desired results.

Do not just focus on preferred or most popular options because those might not be the best ones. The team member needs to determine which option will yield the highest return with the least amount of risk. As a coach, it is wise to ask pointed questions and listen to your team member generate possible options to accomplish these goals. Prompt the team member to generate options that are strategic-level, then move to the tactical and then operational-level details. For example, start with the ways in which the goals, when accomplished, will benefit the organization and the team member. This is the strategic level. Then, explore, at a high-level, paths that the team member can take to accomplish the goals. This is the tactical. And finally, examine the pros and cons of each path in order to identify the option that is most expedient or appropriate. This is the operational level.

Identifying options for accomplishing the goal is just one aspect that a coach will examine in partnership with the team member. A coach will solicit input from the team member to *identify* the tools available, skills, knowledge, networks, and other supports to accomplish the goal. Most importantly, the team member should *decide* on the best resources to draw on to achieve the goal.

Again, the most important thing to remember during this phase of the GROW model is to identify as many options as possible and not to look for *the one* right way. Be innovative and brainstorm with the team member and identify multiple viable options. When choosing the final option to pursue, consider its cost-benefit and risk. The second or third options that were not selected may serve as contingencies, if the first option does not work out as expected.

Now would be a good time to talk about taking risks. The option with the greatest risk is often the one that pays the highest dividends and, of course, may result in the highest losses. It's been pointed out that coaching is the antidote for lack of confidence in performing a task or accomplishing a goal.

Would you guide your team member to select an option that offers more risks instead of safer options?

Well, on the surface, it would seem foolhardy to influence a team member to take risks when that person is already not confident. Imagine sending someone who isn't a confident swimmer into the deepest part of a swimming pool. Viewed another way, selecting a riskier option can build the confidence that some team members need, while others will recoil even further. They key is to know each of your team members and the level of risk each can tolerate.

We discussed in the goal-setting component of the GROW model that a coach should encourage the team member to set stretch goals. The option that a team member chooses might be unexpected or outside of the norm. For example, let's return to the team member who wants to get a position in another department but is conflicted between getting more schooling and adhering to family values. The team member may decide to study on his or her own instead of going to formal classes to get the education needed. This might be considered a risky option, since societal norms dictate that one should have a degree or diploma from an accredited institution to be considered academically qualified. Self-study is not usually recognized as formal education. But for the team member, this is the most cost effective manner and will not take away time from the family. The team member runs the risk of investing time and energy getting educated to become qualified to perform a job only to be overlooked because it requires an accredited degree.

As a coach, you should realize that a team member may choose the option that is more appropriate, based on his or her reality. Some team members will be open to exploring riskier options; others prefer safer ones. Meet your team members where they are. You want to encourage team members to set challenging goals and seek the best options available to accomplish them. And sometimes the option will be to wait or limit the scope of the goal.

So, in summary, your role as a coach is to guide team members through the process of considering options when developing a plan of action to accomplish their goals. Partner with them to consider logical and reasonable possibilities that may materialize when pursuing a goal. These possibilities may enable or be a detriment to goal attainment if they become a reality. The team member must be fully aware of the consequences and be prepared for them.

Consider the amount of time that will be involved and how much time is acceptable for the team member to successfully accomplish the goal or task. Establish a realistic time for the task to be completed—what will the consequences be and what other options will be available if the timeline is not met?

Explore options related to cost—how much will it realistically cost to accomplish the goal or task? Can it be accomplished in a more cost effective manner? What options exist if the team member goes over budget accomplishing the goal?

Very importantly, examine risks with the team member—and explore how to overcome or mitigate them. Discuss resources—identify what resources will be required to accomplish the task or the goal. Are the resources available and, if not, will they be available in time to be of use? All of these topics need to be discussed and clearly understood when discussing the team member's available options.

Once this step is complete, the person you are coaching should have a plan to accomplish the desired goals, or at the least, a solid framework for a plan.

Now, here are useful questions that you can ask when considering options:

- Has a full range of options been identified?
- How will the final option be selected?
- What are the cost-benefits and risks of each option?
- What resources are required for each option?

- Which option represents the best approach?
- Which options should serve as contingencies?

DETERMINING THE WAY FORWARD

The final component of the GROW model is determining the way forward and the motivation, otherwise known as "the will" to persevere and accomplish the desired goal. If you are going to embark on a trip, you need motivation to take it to get to your destination safely and on time. If you are not motivated, you will likely postpone the trip or find some other tasks as distraction. Those you coach will need to make decisions about the paths to take to accomplish their goals, choosing wisely among options and known or future realities. Motivation, however, is the fuel that keeps the team member moving forward.

MOTIVATION

We discussed, for example, setting challenging and SMART goals during the goal-setting phase of the GROW model. The temptation to push team members to stretch and develop advanced skills can also backfire and yield unintended results. Essentially, accomplishing a goal might be demotivating to a team member, if it is too challenging or complex. The team member doesn't spend every day working on the goal; there are other facets of that person's life that must be satisfied. It is very easy for a team member to become overwhelmed by the day-to-day demands of work and personal activities. The team member may also become distracted by new realities or may have just grown weary, especially if the goal takes time to accomplish.

As a coach, your role is to *motivate the team member to accomplish the goals*. The best way to motivate team members is to consistently engage with open and honest communication and be open to maintaining strong interpersonal relationships.

As explained in the *Communicate* section, communication is much more than words; it means being present and engaged both orally and non-verbally and listening attentively to receive and give the right type of feedback. Make sure that goals are clearly understood and the team member is more than capable of completing all necessary tasks, with support from you and others.

An effective coach should also determine whether everyone who is supporting the person you are coaching has the motivation for the journey. Sometimes people who are in support roles can grow weary. Find ways to keep the benefits of accomplishing the goal at the forefront of everyone's mind. Provide reinforcing feedback and recognize all participating team members for their contribution.

As a coach, motivating the team member is not your only responsibility; *help others determine their motivation to achieve the goals*. Make sure team members support each other regardless of the role they are playing in helping the person to accomplish the goal. Guide them towards appreciating the value of teamwork.

One of the best ways to motivate someone to become or remain engaged in accomplishing a goal is to appeal to the WIIFM or What's In It For Me. The team member receiving coaching and those supporting will be able to more readily rally around the goal if they feel they can realize some direct or indirect benefits from the effort. Some team members will be motivated by rewards, like pay increases, public recognition, promotions, and powerful job titles. These are examples of extrinsic motivators. Others will be motivated by the satisfaction of assisting someone to accomplish a goal or just by being of service to others—examples of intrinsic motivators.

As a coach, you will not be able to glean information about what motivates your team members and other supporters, unless you have established a certain level of interpersonal relationship with each person involved on the journey with your team member. As a coach, you want to encourage your team member and others in a support role *to indulge in ongoing self-exploration* by reflecting on the goal at hand and their personal motivation towards accomplishing the goal or supporting its accomplishment.

Even with the most ardent team member who desires to accomplish a goal or task, energy can wane, especially as new or unexpected realties are introduced. Taking time out to reflect and refocus can be a revitalizing effort to maintain the course. The reality is that sometimes self-exploration will require a recalibration of the goal or options, based on new or emerging realities. Remember, the only thing that is constant is change.

Even with the best laid plans, a coach and the team member being coached should expect the unexpected.

So, what if during a coaching relationship, the team member decides to pause or change the course chosen to accomplish the goal?

If your answer is to ask questions and listen to the team member without judgment, then work with the person to examine other options and realities, and then make a decision to refine the goal or maintain momentum, you are correct. This type of thinking shows that you have a handle on how to coach effectively. In order to align with your team member's goals, values and motivation, you need to empower that person to make decisions about how and when to pursue the goal.

Now that we have discussed the Align element and its associated behaviors, let's take a look at a scenario that shows how a supervisor demonstrates the behaviors of this element.

Scenario: Janet is Tim's supervisor. Tim has been in the same position since the company was acquired 15 years ago. Tim is a hard worker, and team members seek him out for guidance often. A year ago, the company introduced new technology to Tim's area. It has taken Tim longer than the other team members to start using the new technology. Tim has demonstrated that he understands how to use the new technology, but does not feel it is more efficient than the old way of performing his tasks. Janet is meeting with Tim for his annual performance review.

Below is an excerpt from the performance review discussion.

Janet: Tim, how are things going with the new software in your area? It's been six months since the Go Live date.

Tim: What software? It's anything but soft. I think you guys missed the mark on this one. I just don't see how this is making my job any easier.

Janet: I hear you clearly that you are not with us on this change. You are not jazzed up about using the software because you don't think it makes your job easier. A number of your teammates tell me that the software is a time saver for them. Why do you think you perceive it differently?

Tim: Well, I've been doing work this way for much longer than everyone else, so I guess I am a pro at doing it this way.

Janet: I agree. You have mastered your role and all the tricks of the trade. Have you thought of this as a new challenge that you can conquer?

Tim: I haven't thought of it that way. But why conquer if you can just live peacefully with what you have? Remember, if it ain't broke, don't fix it.

Align

Janet: The implementation of this new software system is in alignment with our strategic direction, and as members of the team, we want to support the strategic direction of the company to the greatest extent possible. We are in this boat together. Do you want to row in the same direction with us?

Tim: OK, well since you put it that way, I don't want to be a spoil sport. I will spend more time using the system, but I am really concerned that my efficiency will be reduced.

Janet: I understand that it might, but over time you will become even more productive once you master this new software.

Tim: We will definitely need to cross that bridge when we get there.

Janet: So, how do you think you can start using the system and monitor your progress?

Tim: I don't want to be the one to slow down progress. I can set a goal to use the system three days out of the week and keep track of how productive I am with it. I can use it more after I get into the swing of things.

Janet: That's a realistic plan. The goal really is to use the new software every day. Have you thought about how you will get help with the more advanced features of the software?

Tim: I will reach out to some of my teammates. Bob is a techie and seems to really like using the software. I will talk with him first.

Janet: OK, everyone is really busy now that we are down two team members. What if you are not able to gain immediate access to your team members?

Tim: I know that the vendors provide technical support so I can reach out to them.

Janet: OK, please set up at least one weekly meeting with me for the first month to discuss your progress as you transition to using the software efficiently. You have built up too much credibility with your teammates; they look to you as a leader. I don't want to sacrifice that and I know you can master this software.

In this example, Tim had the ability to perform the task, but not the motivation. His supervisor, Janet, was able to motivate him by helping him to understand the value of his contribution to the team and to the organization. Janet used the GROW model to help guide Tim in *setting development goals* that are consistent with the values of the organization. During the meeting, Janet challenged Tim to set *self-improvement goals* and skillfully guided him through the process of *developing strategies* to achieve the goal he has set for himself. Janet also guided Tim to consider the *realities* and *options* that are available for him to accomplish his goal. Janet knows that Tim's *motivation* will wane if the *support structures or resources* are not in place when he needs them. Additionally, Janet encouraged Tim to indulge in *ongoing self-exploration* by setting up weekly progress meetings to reflect and give, as well as receive feedback about his performance. It is also an opportunity for Janet to motivate Tim to ensure that he meets or exceeds performance expectations.

We are almost finished with our discussion of the *Align* element and its behaviors. Here are questions that can help you align with your team members:

- What are the specific steps and timing for each action?
- Do you have the required support and resources?
- What obstacles do you anticipate encountering?
- Do you have the motivation to tackle this initiative?
- What will you do to maintain your motivation level?
- How can you sustain this goal, once achieved?

PERSONAL STORY

Let's review a personal example of when I worked with a team member during a coaching relationship to help realign his career choice with his motivation. The team member reported directly to me when I was responsible for Staffing and Development for a major corporation. He also had an indirect reporting relationship with the leader who was responsible for sales training.

Although the team member excelled at his primary role in my department, he was motivated to work in his part-time sales training role as well. Working in both roles gave him an opportunity to explore and compare them. After two years, he realized that he was more motivated to do the work required by his part-time sales training role.

Realizing that his motivation had become misaligned with the duties required of his primary job, I decided that it was time for me to have a discussion with him. During our discussion, it became clear that he viewed the work in his part-time sales training role as more tangible than the work that he performed in his primary role. So, I asked him how he would feel about moving into the sales training role full time. Although he was ecstatic about the prospect, he still had a few major projects that he needed to complete. He agreed to maintain the status quo until those projects were completed, so we developed a strategy for his transfer to the sales training position once the projects were completed. Several months later, he assumed a full-time sales training role.

Align

The success and the exposure that he achieved performing his sales training role catapulted the team member to several other roles and he continued to be successful. We have maintained a coaching relationship over the years; I mainly function as a sounding board as he continues to grow professionally.

Now that we have come to the end of our discussion of the Align element of the COACH framework, it's your turn to reflect on how well you align with the team members you coach. Take some time to reflect on one or more coaching relationships or coaching discussions you have had. Rate yourself on how well you performed on average, based on the behaviors presented in the self-reflection activity that follows.

SELF-REFLECTION
ALIGN

INSTRUCTIONS

Read each statement below. Use the 0-5 scale to rate yourself on how often you use the behavior described. For example, if you demonstrate the behavior most of the time, enter the number four (4) next to that statement. After you've entered all the scores, add them together and place the raw score total in the Raw Score section of the equation and multiply by two (2) to arrive at your total score. Review the explanation that corresponds with your total score, then read the other explanations.

0	1	2	3	4	5
NEVER	RARELY	SOME-TIMES	HALF THE TIME	MOST TIMES	ALWAYS

YOU ○

21.	Helps others set self-improvement goals.	
22.	Uses models to help others accomplish goals.	

23.	Motivates others to get the job done.	
24.	Encourages others to consider current realities when solving problems.	
25.	Guides others through the process of considering options when developing a plan.	
26.	Helps others determine their motivation to achieve their goals.	
27.	Assists others in setting development goals that are consistent with their values.	
28.	Advises others on developing strategies to achieve career goals.	
29.	Uses a systematic approach to help others grow.	
30.	Encourages ongoing self-exploration.	
	RAW SCORE ⊃	

$X2 =$

RAW SCORE	MULTIPLY BY 2	TOTAL SCORE

79 to 100 (High) — You demonstrate very effective use of the *Align* element behaviors. Inspire and help others develop skills to successfully use them.

65 to 78 (Average) — You demonstrate effective use of the *Align* element behaviors. Continue working to enhance your ability to use them.

Align

Below 65 (Low) — You demonstrate limited use of the *Align* element behaviors. Take advantage of opportunities to enhance your ability to use them.

For a more comprehensive evaluation, a companion COACH[180] assessment is available online. The assessment allows members of your immediate work circle to assess the degree to which you exhibit the behaviors associated with the coaching elements discussed in this book.

Visit **www.AlonzoJohnsonPHD.com** for additional information on how to complete the COACH[180] assessment.

COLLABORATE

"It is literally true that you can succeed best and quickest by helping others to succeed."

— Napoleon Hill

Who are your favorite musical artists? Do they collaborate with other artists?

What do you think about the outcome of these collaboration activities?

Chances are, you think some of the collaboration efforts are successful and others might not be as successful.

Why do artists collaborate with each other?

Could it be to deliver variety or produce a higher quality of sounds to keep fans engaged?

In a coaching relationship, how is collaboration different from or similar to an artist collaborating with another artist?

Actually, it is not that different. In a coaching relationship, collaboration is partnering with the team member to pursue a chosen goal. The outcome from collaborating is similar. The artist—in this case, is the team member who is being coached—wants to produce a much better product by collaborating rather than pursuing a solo project. Sometimes artists may seek out another artist for collaboration to complement their music.

FINDING JOY IN COACHING

As a coach, collaboration is necessary to ensure that the team member being coached has the necessary supports in place to accomplish the goals in the most efficient way possible. When coaches are willing to roll up their sleeves and collaborate with team members to accomplish goals, it provides tangible support and builds credibility and trust. An effective coach should *enjoy working with team members*, whether they are being coached or are offering support.

Finding joy in working with others is sometimes easier said than done, especially in a fast-paced work environment where time is a prized commodity. As we discussed in the *Align* section, coaching takes more time than other leadership development activities, such as training someone. The idea of coaching team members so that they can take on some of the tasks that you currently perform should make coaching well worth spending the time. Finding the time to dedicate to a team member's coaching can be daunting, especially if the goal is complex.

PERSONAL PREFERENCES

Another circumstance that may not be considered joyful is coaching others who do not prefer this type of one-on-one exchange or even engaging others to support them in accomplishing their goals. You may also have misgivings about engaging at this level with a team member.

So how can a coaching relationship last if the coach or the person being coached prefers not to engage so intimately or work so closely with other team members?

As a coach, you are a leader first—you've accepted the role to lead others and, as we've discussed throughout this book, coaching is arguably among the most meaningful ways to lead. When you are in a leadership role, your preference becomes less of a priority than the needs of those who look to you for development and guidance.

For the team member being coached, who prefers not to work with others, your duty as a coach is to instill the virtues of teamwork and hold that team member accountable for contributing to the team. A coach should never insist that team members ditch their personalities and adapt to the coaching *rules or expectations* that are set or implied by the coach. While you may expect for the team member to work as part of the team, the coaching relationship should be designed around the needs and desires of the team member. For example, a coach should not force one-on-one meetings if the team member just prefers a periodic check-in email.

We spent time in the first few sections discussing that a strong coaching relationship cannot exist in a vacuum; it has to be built on a foundation of open and honest communication and strong interpersonal skills. A coach should be deliberate about understanding the personality preferences of every team member so that meaningful coaching relationships can occur.

THE VALUE OF COLLABORATION IN COACHING

Collaboration in coaching does not happen just between the coach and the team member you are coaching. Collaboration requires the collective energies of everyone who can contribute to the success of the team member. It allows each person involved in supporting the team member's goal to contribute by lending their expertise, sharing ideas, providing constructive feedback, and challenging the team member to accomplish the goal in the most efficient and dynamic way possible.

Effective collaboration fuels creative problem-solving and decision-making. When you collaborate or arrange collaborative relationships with the team member, you are reinforcing trust and demonstrating a genuine desire to add value to the team member's cause. Coaching is not about solving problems and making decisions for your team members. It is really about laying the foundation and *encouraging others to find solutions to their problems* and make sound decisions. A coach should be able to collaborate with the team member without taking on the tasks that the person should be performing.

So the question is how can a coach collaborate if the decision-making, problem-solving and other tasks are the responsibility of the team member?

Collaboration can take many forms. To support the team members, the coach may need to exert physical energy, such as providing hands-on assistance to complete a task. The coach may take an indirect approach to collaborate by assisting the team member to come up with a strategy to accomplish the task or goal. In another instance, the coach may influence others to help the team member make progress on the desired goal.

Collaboration in coaching could be viewed in this analogy. You, the coach, are a passenger in a vehicle driven by the team member who is being coached. The team member knows how to drive but is not an expert. On this trip, both the coach and the team member are fully aware of the destination and the road blocks or barriers that might impede the journey. You are in the car as a driving partner, who is eager to help the team member select the best route, stop at the gas stations with the best-priced fuel or identify rest stop choices. You may even pump the gas, but all the decisions that are to be made on the trip are left up to the driver—the team member. Although, you are a more experienced driver and may influence the decisions along the way, the final decisions rest with the driver.

It should be clear to you by now that coaching relationships rarely end with just the coach and the team member working together; others usually get involved. In coaching, the coach plays an active role in ensuring that the team member builds synergies with other team members who are offering support by tapping into their strengths.

REMOVING BARRIERS TO EFFECTIVE COLLABORATION

The coach should also remove barriers to productive collaboration. As a coach, *you will strive to help your team member to achieve his or her goals by encouraging collaboration and promoting cooperation*, while facilitating the *exchange of learning, best practices and new ideas*. A coach helps team members *assess their skills and come up with ways to broaden them*. In order to be an effective collaborator, a coach must *treat others fairly*, while helping everyone who is involved in the coaching relationship *to identify unproductive behaviors and eliminate them*.

Let's spend some time examining these behaviors in greater detail. When you collaborate, you will assume multiple roles as discussed in this section. You will likely become a gate keeper, who keeps distractions away from the team member so that the focus will be on the goal. A coach may play the role of advocate, devil's advocate, sounding board, cheerleader, among other roles. The ability to perform different roles requires a lot of flexibility. These roles are also not static and may even evolve from day-to-day based on the situation. The only constant is that your ultimate goal, regardless of role, is to *strive to help your team member to achieve goals by encouraging collaboration and promoting cooperation.*

As the quote goes, "No man is an island...." A coach must influence team members to seek the resources needed and use the right people skills to influence others to collaborate and cooperate with each other to achieve the desired goal. The ability to collaborate and promote cooperation may not come naturally for everyone, including the coach and the team member being coached.

So what happens in a coaching relationship when the coach, the team member being coached, or both have little or no interest in collaborating with others to accomplish a goal?

Both the coach and the team member are engaging in a leadership practice. Coaching should be an empowering experience for both, and it should challenge the team member to explore unknown or less familiar paths in order to accomplish goals. Remember our discussion in the *Align* section about realistic or relevant goals? A person who has a preference for displaying a certain behavior should not be pigeonholed and be guided to accomplish goals or tasks that fit that person's preference. The coach should challenge the team member to reach out to unfamiliar sources for assistance and promote cooperation among team members who have different work attitudes, values or perspectives.

LEARNING THROUGH COLLABORATION

Once the team member and others in supporting roles have bought into the vision, an effective coach should *facilitate the exchange of learning, best practices and new ideas.* The reason for building and maintaining collaborative relationships in coaching is to allow everyone involved in the process to learn—yes, the coach should also learn from the experience. Learning is a critical component in coaching and can occur through planned or unplanned learning events. In other words, we are learning all the time, regardless of whether we choose to do so. In coaching, the learning experience might be structured so that the learning is more intentional, but it can also happen when we're not even thinking about it.

Regardless of how learning occurs, the coach, the team member being coached and other supporting team members should be open to learning from each other and through each other, using collaboration as a vehicle. As mentioned in this section, collaboration spurs curiosity and creativity because each member has some unique perspectives to offer. When brilliant ideas and best practices are presented, the outcome will yield benefits not just for the team member being coached but for everyone who is involved.

BROADENING SKILLS THROUGH COLLABORATION

In a coaching relationship, a coach is not presented with a tabula rasa or blank slate, as far as knowledge, skills and abilities are concerned. A team member comes to the coaching experience with skills and knowledge. These might not be refined and the team member's confidence might not be high. A coach's task is to collaborate in a way that allows team members to conduct ongoing self-reflection and *assess their skills and come up with ways to broaden them.*

The ultimate measure of success for a coach and the team member is not just about accomplishing a goal or task, but the amount of personal and professional growth that can be attributed directly to the coaching relationship. The coach, the team member and other supporters realize meaningful growth from the collaborative experience.

What does growth look like in a collaborative coaching relationship?

As we've discussed throughout this book, the reason a coach collaborates with team members in a coaching relationship is to help accomplish a desired goal; this is a deliberate or expected outcome. However, there will be additional outcomes that are not so deliberate. In the Open element discussion about the Johari Window, four panes represent how we are viewed— the Open, Blind Spot, Hidden and Unknown panes. If the goal is challenging enough and all involved are encouraged to broaden their skills and remain open to learning best practices, you as a coach will have created the fertile conditions for everyone to work together and excel well beyond what they thought possible. In other words, through collaboration, team members will motivate each other to explore untapped talents that otherwise would have remained hidden.

UNINTENDED BENEFITS OF COLLABORATING

Collaborating with others to gain the confidence or motivation to accomplish technical tasks or goals is often the focus of coaching relationships. Oftentimes, the behavioral or soft skills—communicating, teaming, negotiating, handling conflict—that are used to carry out the technical skills are not considered. The lack of effective soft skills may negatively impact the accomplishment of the goal or task. Team members who collaborate with others in a coaching environment have the opportunity to develop or improve soft skills.

A number of tools can be used to provide the coach, team member and other supporters with insights into how well they deploy soft skills. Many of these tools promote collaboration and honest feedback from people who have observed team members' behaviors over time.

The COACH[180] assessment, a companion assessment for this book, is an example of such a tool. Coaches can use the tool to solicit feedback from others. Doing so helps coaches to determine the extent to which they are displaying the right coaching behaviors. As mentioned throughout this book, coaching is a form of leadership. The LEAD 360, Emotional Quotient-Inventory 2.0® (EQ-i 2.0®) and other tools can be used to assess leadership skills and identify performance gaps. Doing so will help the coach, the team member and others to identify and improve soft skills and reap unexpected benefits from the coaching relationship. The coach should encourage everyone on a coaching journey, regardless of the role, to continuously engage in feedback, self-discovery and self-disclosure so that they can become well-rounded professionals.

PROMOTING THE RIGHT BEHAVIORS

To encourage collaboration, a coach must *treat others fairly* so that team members can accomplish their goal and excel professionally and personally. As a coach, you will need to act impartially, without any hidden agendas. So what does treating others fairly look like in a coaching relationship?

Treating others fairly means that a coach should not thrust opinions, preferences or values on the team member being coached or other team members who have assumed supporting roles. Everyone who is collaborating to accomplish a goal may not be thrilled with every decision the team member makes. A coach will stifle collaboration by conjuring ways to change the trajectory of events when a plan is made and is being executed. Sometimes a coach may need to influence a change when the reason is bona fide.

You might be wondering when it would be bona fide to *influence* a change of plans. As we discussed earlier, change happens. As also discussed in the *Align* section, a PESTEL analysis can reveal political, economic, social, technological, environmental or legal changes that can negatively impact goal attainment. Even daily operational changes can impact the outcome of a goal. A coach may have more strategic insights than a team member and therefore has the ability to *read the tea leaves* and identify realities that may negatively impact the accomplishment of the goal. As a coach, you must be able to help the team member navigate landmines in order to accomplish the goal efficiently and grow professionally, while still fostering a spirit of collaboration. A coach may not be able to provide a specific reason for guiding the team member in another direction due to confidentiality, ethics and other constraints. For example, the coach may be aware of leadership's decision to consolidate resources from two departments and form a single department. The coach is not allowed to share this news with anyone. Your team member is working hard to get a position in the department that will be impacted and other team members are taking on additional duties to support their colleague's transition. The coach has to influence a change or modification to the goal and maintain a collaborative environment without divulging company secrets.

As discussed, an effective coaching relationship requires trust. A coach should be able to withhold sensitive information from everyone who is on the coaching journey without any negative impact to trust and collaboration.

AVOIDING UNPRODUCTIVE BEHAVIORS

Even in a highly trusting and collaborative coaching environment, the team member being coached might not agree with you or see things your way. As emphasized throughout this book, it is incumbent on a coach to offer guidance and allow the team member to decide on the *right* path to take. The team member's right path may be different from yours because you may have information that is not available to the team member being coached or other supporting members. In the *Leading Made Easy* book, one of the most powerful principles is *Learn from Mistakes.* You are actually leading and inculcating leadership skills and encouraging trust and collaboration when you allow team members to learn from mistakes that they have made or have observed others making. Allow the team member to take risks and *fail safely.* In other words, as a coach, you should not allow team members to pursue a path that will make goal attainment impossible. That is why it is important when you are in a coaching relationship to identify *unproductive behaviors and eliminate them.* An example of unproductive behavior on a collaborative team would be group think. This occurs when team members make poor decisions for the sake of having a harmonious and collaborative relationship. Other forms of unproductive behaviors include making impulsive decisions, not being open to the feedback from others, lack of commitment, motivation, accountability, or conflict management skills.

So how does a coach identify and eliminate unproductive behaviors that sabotage collaboration?

You cannot identify something that you are not aware of or that is unfamiliar to you—so you need to continuously monitor your team. You should be able to identify the correct behaviors and develop them within your team. You should know the baseline performance of your team and consistently monitor performance of all team members, including those who are involved in the coaching relationship.

When there is a change that may negatively impact the performance of the team, your duty as a coach is to let your team members know what the behavior is, the potential impact of the behavior, the consequences that may result, and reinforce the desired behavior. As discussed in the *Communicate* section of this book, this is called redirecting feedback.

On the flip side, your continuous monitoring could reveal that the team, including the team member being coached, is collaborating effectively and meeting or exceeding performance standard. You are obligated to let the team member and others who are collaborating with the team member know what is happening. Let them know the positive impact that the behaviors have on the outcomes. This is providing reinforcing feedback. This type of feedback was also examined in the *Communicate* section of the book. When you provide genuine reinforcing feedback, it makes it easier for you to provide redirecting feedback when things are not going so well.

Accomplishing the goal of the team member you are coaching is the priority. Through collaborating, team members gain confidence because they feel that you are on their side. This also goes a long way towards building trust and confidence.

Let's take a moment to review how Jerry collaborated with his team member.

Scenario: Jerry, a team lead, has asked his team members to come up with a more efficient way of visualizing the monthly reports. The goal is to increase the number of people who view and use the data in the report to make business decisions. Team members have come up with three ideas. Jerry has asked them to choose one of those ideas to present to him. He puts team member, Gwen, in charge of working with the team to accomplish this task. Gwen has agreed to guide the team to consensus.

Below is the transcript from Gwen and Jerry's status update meeting.

Jerry: Good morning Gwen. It's about time for us to decide on how to increase viewership of our unit reports. What's the verdict?

Gwen: We have not been able to obtain consensus.

Jerry: Why?

Gwen: The team members are not willing to accept other members' ideas.

Jerry: The goal is for you to collaborate with your team members and come up with the best path forward. We really need to find a way to engage our internal customers and get some visibility for the work we do as a unit, especially now that sales are down. What are you going to do to get us to that point?

Gwen: I'm not sure. I thought it would be easy to reach a consensus, but I do not want to isolate anyone. Maybe I could meet with team members individually and conduct a "pros and cons" activity with each idea and let them choose the option that has more pros. Then send an email letting everyone know the option that was selected.

Jerry: That's a good idea. How do you ensure that team members will feel that the selection process was transparent if you were to choose that approach?

Gwen: Oh yeah, some may feel that the selection process was not conducted fairly. What if I conducted the pros and cons activity with everyone and select the idea with the most pros?

Jerry: That sounds like a more collaborative approach. This approach might take longer than meeting with them individually. How will you accomplish this, given everyone's hectic schedule and how passionate everyone feels about this topic?

Gwen: I will work with their assistants and set up a one-hour brainstorming session and emphasize before the session that a decision must be made during that session, so they should come to the session prepared. They will have the worksheet at least a week before the session.

Jerry: I look forward to reviewing the final result.

In this example, Jerry, the team lead, assigned his team member a task to accomplish and learned that the team member is having a hard time gaining consensus. Jerry's approach was to collaborate with the team member to come up with an approach that would work for the team and that Gwen felt comfortable executing. Jerry also encouraged Gwen to collaborate with the other team members to accomplish the task. In this example, Jerry did not physically assist Gwen with accomplishing the task; he had a conversation with her. Jerry asked the right questions to get Gwen to think about *options* and *realities* as she planned to accomplish the task.

Jerry demonstrated that he wanted Gwen to take ownership of the task and encouraged her to find solutions. He also encouraged Gwen to achieve her goals by *encouraging collaboration and promoting cooperation*. Gwen facilitated a brainstorming session, which allowed for the *exchange of learning, best practices and new ideas*. It is not immediately clear that Gwen thought she had the skills to influence her team members. Jerry, her coach, helped her to *assess her skills*, and as a result of being guided through a series of probing questions, Gwen was able to develop more confidence to collaborate and influence her team members in more ways than she thought possible.

Lack of consensus or commitment on a team is another example of *unproductive behavior* that needs to be eliminated; it is known as a dysfunction. Jerry, being an insightful team lead was eager to eliminate it from the team. He tapped Gwen to work with her team to eliminate the behavior. Not only was he able to eliminate the unproductive behavior, he was able to coach and support Gwen as she gained valuable leadership skills. As discussed, your role as a coach is not to fix things for your team members; it's about empowering them to rise to the occasion and deliver top performance at all times.

PERSONAL STORY

I'd like to share a personal example of how I collaborated with a team member to accomplish a goal.

The team member, who reported directly to me, set a long-term goal of becoming a Human Resources Generalist. The planning to complete this goal necessitated that she set a series of intermediate goals. One of those intermediate goals required her to complete a college degree in Human Resources. Although the team member and I agreed that a degree in Human Resources wasn't required for the career change, we thought that the degree would better position her to land the position and provide her with a solid foundation for a career in Human Resources.

The team member initially made steady progress towards earning her degree, according to the timeline that she had established as part of her goal. However, progress began to wane as she neared the completion of the general studies component that was required for the degree. My assessment was that this lack of progress was due to two obstacles: a loss of motivation and finances. I knew, from experience, that once a student quit school, it could be very challenging to start back again, so I decided to intervene.

After sharing my concern with the team member, we explored options that would allow her to continue her studies. We agreed that the way forward would be for me to require her, as part of the company's performance management process, to complete the English course that she needed for her general studies—and I did. This action not only reignited her motivation to continue her program but also led to the company funding the course that she needed from a different source. This collaborative effort resulted in the team member staying in school and completing her degree on schedule. And yes, she did change careers and eventually landed that Human Resources Generalist position.

Now that we have come to the end of our discussion on the *Collaborate* element of the COACH framework, it's your turn to reflect on how well you collaborate as a coach. And how well do you display the behaviors associated with the element in your coaching relationships? Take some time to reflect on one or more coaching relationships or discussions you have had. Rate yourself on how well you performed on average, based on the behaviors listed in the self-reflection activity that follows.

SELF-REFLECTION
COLLABORATE

INSTRUCTIONS

Read each statement below. Use the 0-5 scale to rate yourself on how often you use the behavior described. For example, if you demonstrate the behavior most of the time, enter the number four (4) next to that statement. After you've entered all the scores, add them together and place the raw score total in the Raw Score section of the equation and multiply by two (2) to arrive at your total score. Review the explanation that corresponds with your total score, then read the other explanations.

0	1	2	3	4	5
NEVER	RARELY	SOME-TIMES	HALF THE TIME	MOST TIMES	ALWAYS

YOU ()

31.	Strives to promote cooperation.	
32.	Helps others recognize and eliminate unproductive behavior.	

33.	Encourages others to find their own solutions to problems.	
34.	Helps others assess their skills and determine how to broaden them.	
35.	Enjoys working with others.	
36.	Achieves goals through collaboration.	
37.	Encourages collaboration.	
38.	Challenges others to broaden their thinking.	
39.	Treats others fairly.	
40.	Facilitates the exchange of learning, best practices, and new ideas.	
	RAW SCORE ⮕	

X2 =

| RAW SCORE | MULTIPLY BY 2 | TOTAL SCORE |

79 to 100 (High) — You demonstrate very effective use of the *Collaborate* element behaviors. Inspire and help others develop skills to successfully use it.

65 to 78 (Average) — You demonstrate effective use of the *Collaborate* element behaviors. Continue working to enhance your ability to use it.

Below 65 (Low) — You demonstrate limited use of the *Collaborate* element behaviors. Take advantage of opportunities to enhance your ability to use it.

Collaborate

For a more comprehensive evaluation, a companion COACH¹⁸⁰ assessment is available online. The assessment allows members of your immediate work circle to assess the degree to which you exhibit the behaviors associated with the coaching elements discussed in this book.

Visit **www.AlonzoJohnsonPHD.com** for additional information on how to complete the COACH¹⁸⁰ assessment.

HARNESS

"There is no heavier burden than an unfulfilled potential."

— Charles Schulz

What is your mental model of the word *harness*? Do you think of a horse fitted in a way to be controlled or manipulated by a person? In an effective coaching relationship, there is no control or manipulation between the coach and the team member receiving the coaching. What a coach strives to do consistently is to allow that team member to *discover hidden talents that he or she possesses* and leverage them to achieve positive outcomes.

In other words, an effective coach must be able to identify the strengths that team members possess, help them to acknowledge them, and then guide them towards harnessing those strengths in meaningful ways. In coaching, harnessing simply means that the coach strives at all times to bring out the best in the team member.

THE BLIND SPOT REVISITED

Earlier in the *Open* section of the book, we started the discussion about blind spots and other facets of our being that have not yet been fully explored. A coach should help the team member to unearth hidden talents. Here again, we see that for a coach to harness the potential of the team member, a relationship has to be fully established. The coach has to truly know the team member and be genuinely interested in that person's success in order to identify the qualities that make that team member unique.

In realizing the potential in others, coaches have to help team members *map their own development path*. Becoming aware of a strength or talent is usually a very enriching experience for a team member. Oftentimes, that person may not yet know how to leverage that strength in meaningful or rewarding ways. Left alone, the team member may derail personally or professionally if the new found strength or talent is used in misguided ways. For example, a team member may possess charisma and may use it to dissuade other team members from following company policy. A good coach should be willing to *collaborate* with the team member and come up with strategies that, when implemented, will provide the right exposure that highlight and reward talent.

FOUNDATIONAL COACHING TOOLS REVISITED

Throughout this book, we have discussed the most basic, yet important tools that coaches have at their disposal to guide, challenge and stimulate team members who are being coached: listening and asking questions. A coach should encourage team members to reflect and discover their talents. In other words, a coach should place the team member being coached in situations that will allow that person to gain awareness of these strengths and talents.

Coaches should know how to *ask questions to guide the thinking of team members*. An effective coach knows how to ask questions and uses this technique to influence positive outcomes.

In the *Communicate* section, we discussed the types of questions and the questioning techniques that are used to elicit rich information or prompt a desired action. An effective coach understands the type of questions to ask and when to ask them. Most importantly, the coach knows the importance of listening to the answers. You, as the coach, may already know the potential of the team member and may want to refine a particular skill or talent. But you want the team member to make decisions and discover hidden talents independently.

So, what is the best type of question to ask if you are aware of a skill or talent that is not yet apparent to the team member you are coaching?

You will get more insight from the team member if you ask open-ended questions to allow time to think, reflect and respond more expansively. For example, a coach may have observed that a team member has the ability to influence others, and believes that she would do well in a leadership role. On occasion the coach has asked the team member to assume the team lead role temporarily even though the person has never shared any leadership role ambition. The team member usually performs every time she is asked to lead the team.

How would you as a coach broach the idea of the team member serving in a leadership role?

First, you would want to find out the team member's understanding of leadership and the prospect of performing the role. You may want to start out with a general topic on leadership by using open-ended questions to get the team leader's perspective on the topic. Then, depending on the level of interpersonal relationship you have developed, you may want to discuss career aspirations. Engaging in this type of conversation too early may cause the person undue stress because as human beings, we are wired to think the worst. If the coach engages at that level too early, the team member may feel that her position on the team is being threatened.

During your discussion with the team member whose leadership skill you want to harness, the topic of taking on a leadership role may not emerge as a developmental path for her.

You know that the leadership skill exists, so you should assess the will or motivation and then decide whether to harness that leadership potential and help her uncover her strength.

The question then arises, what if the team member does not possess the motivation to ascend to a leadership role? Would you still assign that person a temporary leadership role?

The answer is—it depends. As part of harnessing a team member's potential, you have to ask probing questions and listen attentively to find out the cause of the lack of motivation. Once you fully understand the realities, you will take the most beneficial route to develop the team member.

EMPOWERING TEAM MEMBERS

There might be times when a team member possesses the skill and the motivation but lacks the confidence. What do you do in that case?

You will *empower your team member to achieve his or her goals*. One of the most empowering things that you can do as a coach is to provide *clarity* around the goal. As discussed in the *Align* section, sometimes all the team members you are coaching need to boost their confidence is to clearly understand the goal, its benefits and what it will take to accomplish it.

Another empowering task that the coach should complete to harness potential is to *offer ongoing support* to team members as they work to achieve goals and discover hidden potential. Support means offering the resources that each team member needs to accomplish the goal. As Isaac Newton put it, "If I have seen further than others, it is by *standing upon the shoulders of giants.*" Throwing your full support behind the team members you coach will unleash their hidden potential and build trust, confidence and loyalty. Even if your team members fail initially to accomplish the goal, they will be empowered to persevere because of your support.

We discussed different types of resources or supports in the *Align* section. You can harness team members' potential when you coach them by providing a safe space for them to try new approaches. We also discussed that a coach plays various roles throughout the coaching relationship. You can support the team member by just being a sounding board. Influence team members to access the right supports at the right time to facilitate their professional or personal growth.

Another empowering experience that a coach should introduce to the coaching relationship is *autonomy*. As discussed throughout this book, coaching isn't about doing for team members what they can do for themselves. As a coach, make sure team members are comfortable making decisions and taking actions towards accomplishing their goals. A part of encouraging autonomy is fostering the ability of the team member to take risks. Smart risk-taking is a leadership skill that a coach must help team members develop. Allow your team member to take risks and learn from them, while working autonomously and gaining experience.

Let's discus *giving recognition* as an empowering tool that a coach can use to motivate team members to think creatively and venture out of their comfort zones to discover their strengths and talents. As the saying goes, "encouragement sweetens labor"; recognize your team members when there is an opportunity to do so. Giving recognition is a form of reinforcing feedback. As a coach, you let team members know that you recognize the value or significance of what they have accomplished. It is a way of encouraging your team members to be even more innovative in their professional and personal pursuits. As a coach, you are not expected to recognize team members with lavish gifts or rewards, although a modest gift usually is a nice touch. Find ways to let the team members you coach know that you are paying attention to their performance and you not only appreciate, but are in full support of the direction they have taken. Tangible forms of recognition like gifts and other rewards are good, but sometimes a full-throated acknowledgement and praise can go a long way to encourage a team member to excel.

When you provide clear guidance, support and recognition, you are *enabling your team member to act*. Think about how children gain confidence when their parents are actively involved in their lives and show them that they believe in them. In the same way, team members will be empowered to take calculated risks to accomplish a goal when they feel you "have their backs."

INFLUENCING TEAM MEMBERS

As a coach, you lead by *guiding team members to discover their full potential* by helping them *identify strengths and opportunities for growth.* Your job as a coach is to help your team members to indulge in continuous self-reflection and look for growth opportunities that spark their interests and align with their professional or personal goals. Once team members have decided on a path to professional growth, help them to stay motivated by reinforcing the benefits of accomplishing the goal and keep the focus on current and emerging realities, and options that are available to them. Along the way, observe the team members' performance and challenge them to set goals that will transform them as professionals.

Influence your team members to accomplish the goals they have set. Most people start out with goals; then, life happens, and many goals are either set aside or forgotten. Remind team members that it is never too late to accomplish both personal and professional goals. Use the GROW model introduced in the *Align* section to help them explore current realities that may be impeding the accomplishment of the goal and the options that exist. Establish checkpoints so that you can track progress towards accomplishing the desired goal. As established many times in this book, trust is important to developing great coaching relationships. If your team members trust you, they know that they can rely on you for objective performance feedback and guidance. A trusting relationship with you will motivate team members and provide them the reassurance that they need to make bold moves towards accomplishing their most ambitious goals, whether professional or personal ones.

ENCOURAGE LEARNING

Human beings are creatures of habit. As a result, it is very easy for us to do the things we have always done because it feels comfortable and safe. *Encourage your team member to learn new ways of doing things.* Learning new ways of doing things involves risks. And we already know that taking risks is a leadership behavior. The best way to encourage out-of-the box thinking and performance is to coach by example. As a coach, you may lose credibility if you guide team members to set ambitious goals and pursue unconventional means to harness their talents to accomplish their goals, and you cannot point to one example of when you made a similar effort.

While you may not be able to draw from personal experience in every coaching situation, you should be able to draw on significant depth and breadth of experience. Being a leader is not a title; you should demonstrate leadership skills whenever and wherever the opportunity presents itself. You may be born with the natural ability to lead or you may have received help to harness that skill. You may have learned leadership skills as part of your professional growth and development. Regardless of how you acquired your leadership skills, use the experience you've gained to help guide the decisions and actions of your team members. You can also draw from other people's experience. Therefore, as a coach, you must be intellectually curious and stay informed of past, present and emerging trends so that you can be the sounding board for the team member who wants to try new ways of doing things.

Undoubtedly, even famous people with talents have failed. Failing at some point is inevitable. Your team members will only be able to harness their skills and talents through trial and error. Support your team member by sharing your failings and that of others who have had significant setbacks but persevered. Challenge your team member to excel, even when it appears as if failure is the only option. When challenged, people will usually meet and often surpass expectations. Treat your team members as creative human beings with the ability to make decisions and successfully accomplish any goal. Create an environment in which team members are eager to learn and experiment with new ideas; demonstrate unwavering confidence in your team members' ability to excel.

Here is a scenario in which Tony, the coach, is working with team member Joan. Tony wants Joan to gain confidence in speaking up in meetings and sharing her ideas.

Scenario: Joan is a seasoned member of the team. She complements the team well with her great analytical skills. Joan is observant and does not speak up in meetings or during problem-solving sessions. Last week, Joan emailed her boss, Tony, with her concerns about a decision that was made during the team meeting. Tony is considering Joan for a promotion to supervisor. He wants her to start asserting herself more in order to be an effective leader. Tony meets with Joan for a one-on-one discussion.

Tony: Joan, thank you for sharing your concern about the decision we made during the meeting last week. We are fortunate to have you on our team, Joan. The skills you bring to the team have improved our performance. I have noticed that you don't speak up during meetings. The team made a decision at our last meeting and you emailed me your concerns after the meeting ended. Sharing your insight during the meeting would have been helpful to the team. Help me understand your reservation about speaking up in meetings.

Joan: Well, I prefer to listen more than I speak.

Tony: Yes, it is usually better to listen than speak. Do you think it was better to listen rather than share your thoughts during the meeting last week?

Joan: I suppose not. I didn't think my concerns were legitimate enough to share with anyone else but you.

Tony: Why do you think that?

Joan: I don't know. I just don't want to embarrass myself, I guess.

Tony: So, what I'm hearing is that you are not confident that your ideas have enough merit, and your team members may think less of you, if you risk sharing them. Is that correct?

Joan: Yeah. Who wants that?

Tony: Why do you think, as part of the team, your fellow team members would have a negative view of you for sharing an idea?

Joan: Because that happened at a place I used to work.

Tony: You have great ideas and your perspectives are important to the team. I understand your misgivings for speaking up based on your past experience. My team and I have worked really hard to create an environment in which every team member can share ideas freely. As one of the members of the team, I believe you will realize that every team member's opinion counts. The fact that you've shared your opinion with me is a good first step. I want you to get comfortable sharing your ideas with your team members. How do you think you can start getting comfortable sharing information with your team members and others?

Joan: Maybe I can start sharing with team members I am more comfortable engaging with, and eventually I can share ideas with the larger team.

Tony: That's a good plan. When do you plan to start and who specifically are you planning to start with?

Joan: Maria and Sam are pretty cool and we work together more often. I can start bouncing ideas off them and then ask them to support me in the meetings if I have to say something.

Tony: OK. How can I support you?

In this scenario, Tony was able to get Joan to commit to speaking up more in meetings by guiding her to get the support she needs to *enable her to act*. The coach guided her to take a path that would help her to discover her *full potential* and *identify her strength and opportunities for growth*. Joan brings good analytical skills to the team, but her lack of confidence gets in the way of her team benefiting from that skill. Keeping quiet in meetings does not afford Joan the opportunity to leverage the skill and showcase her talent to the team. Demonstrating this skill would open the door to more opportunity for Joan to use and become even more adept at using her talent.

Joan's supervisor, Tony, sees leadership abilities in her, but judging from Joan's behavior, she does not feel that she is able to influence her team members. During the meeting, Tony asked questions to guide Joan's decision, listened to Joan's responses, and sought clarification to understand the reason Joan is not comfortable. The coach opened the door to offering support to Joan in order to bring out the best in her.

PERSONAL STORY

Here is a personal example in which I was able to harness the skills and talent of a team member.

I once hired a young intern just out of graduate school who reported to work on his first day with unkempt attire. His shirt was untucked and wrinkled; this violated the company's dress policy. I realized that he had no experience navigating the corporate world; so, after welcoming him to the team, I offered him redirective feedback concerning his attire. This feedback was the catalyst for many coaching discussions that followed over the years.

Of course, this young intern required more redirective feedback and mentoring than coaching at first. However, as he gained more experience in his role, he was eager to set stretch-goals to continue growing in his role and was extremely receptive to being coached to achieve success. The personal and professional growth that he realized through coaching is admirable and is exemplary of the *Harness* element that we discussed in this section. As of the publication of this book, the team member has risen to an executive level role, within a prominent company and is responsible for organizational development across the United States.

We have come to the end of our discussion on the *Harness* element of the COACH framework. Now, it's your turn to reflect on your harnessing skills as a coach and how well you display the Harness behaviors in your coaching relationships.

Take some time to reflect on one or more coaching relationships or discussions you have had. Rate yourself on how well you performed on average, based on the behaviors listed in the self-reflection activity that follows.

SELF-REFLECTION

HARNESS

INSTRUCTIONS

Read each statement below. Use the 0-5 scale to rate yourself on how often you use the behavior described. For example, if you demonstrate the behavior most of the time, enter the number four (4) next to that statement. After you've entered all the scores, add them together and place the raw score total in the Raw Score section of the equation and multiply by two (2) to arrive at your total score. Review the explanation that corresponds with your total score, then read the other explanations.

0	1	2	3	4	5
NEVER	RARELY	SOME-TIMES	HALF THE TIME	MOST TIMES	ALWAYS

YOU ⊍

41.	Guides others towards goal achievement.	
42.	Brings out the best in others.	

43.	Helps others map their development paths.	
44.	Uses questions to guide the thinking of others.	
45.	Empowers others to achieve goals.	
46.	Enables others to act.	
47.	Guides others to discover their full potential.	
48.	Helps others identify their strength and growth opportunities.	
49.	Influences individuals to accomplish goals.	
50.	Encourages others to learn new ways of doing things.	
	RAW SCORE ⇨	

$X2=$

RAW SCORE	MULTIPLY BY 2	TOTAL SCORE

79 to 100 (High) — You demonstrate very effective use of the *Harness* element behaviors. Inspire and help others develop skills to successfully use them.

65 to 78 (Average) — You demonstrate effective use of the *Harness* element behaviors. Continue working to enhance your ability to use them.

Below 65 (Low) — You demonstrate limited use of the *Harness* element behaviors. Take advantage of opportunities to enhance your ability to use them.

For a more comprehensive evaluation, a companion COACH[180] assessment is available online. The assessment allows members of your immediate work circle to assess the degree to which you exhibit the behaviors associated with the coaching elements discussed in this book.

Visit **www.AlonzoJohnsonPHD.com** for additional information on how to complete the COACH[180] assessment.

CONCLUSION

In this book, we explored the five elements of effective coaching: **C**ommunicate, **O**pen, **A**lign, **C**ollaborate and **H**arness. Coaching, while used informally, is a much-underutilized tool in the leader's tool bag. In order for an organization to sustain its success, a strong coaching culture needs to be developed.

The art of coaching takes more time than other leadership tasks. However, the return is greater when compared to other forms of leadership activities that are deployed in organizations and in everyday life. Coaching is a contact form of leadership, which causes some leaders to become squeamish about engaging their team members in a coaching relationship.

The five elements presented in this book are meant to provide a framework for anyone who wants to enrich the life of someone else through coaching. The *Communicate* element takes up a significant portion of the book and for a very good reason: all the other elements depend on effective communication skills to be deployed efficiently. Effective communication is the pillar of effective coaching. The common threads that flow from the *Communicate* element to the others are effective listening, questioning, feedback and interpersonal skills.

Throughout the book, other models, tools and techniques are presented to help coaches have more effective coaching relationships. As the author of this book, my goal is to provide a framework for leaders, whether or not they are in a formal leadership role, to constantly think about coaching someone towards excellence. And when there is an opportunity to coach, do so boldly with this book as your resource. This book was also written to empower organizational leaders to include coaching as a strategic approach to sustaining or improving organizational performance.

For anyone who dares to engage in such a noble leadership task as coaching, this book is for you.

SUGGESTED READINGS

Bariso, Justin. *EQ Applied: The Real-World Guide to Emotional Intelligence.* Borough Hall, 2018.

Canfield, Jack and Chee, Peter. *Coaching for Breakthrough Success: Proven Techniques for Making Impossible Dreams Possible.* McGraw-Hill Education, 2013.

De la Maza, Michael and Argue Brock. *Agile Coaching: Wisdom from Practitioners.* CreateSpace Independent Publishing Platform, 2017.

Greenleaf, Robert K. *The Servant as Leader.* The Greenleaf Center for Servant Leadership, 2015.

Johnson, Alonzo. *Leading Made Easy: Four Principles for Leadership Effectiveness.* OASYS Press, 2016.

Landsberg, Max. *The Tao of Coaching: Boost Your Effectiveness at Work by Inspiring and Developing Those Around You.* Profile Books, 2015.

McMahon, Gladeana and Leimon, Averil. *Performance Coaching for Dummies.* John Wiley & Sons, Ltd., 2008.

Richards, Serena. *Leadership Coaching: Leading at The Edge: Inspire, Persuade, Influence, Gain Power and Trust.* Amazon Digital Services LLC, 2015.

Richards, Serena. *Performance Coaching: A Complete Guide for Growing Human Potential and Purpose.* CreateSpace Independent Publishing Platform, 2015.

Stanier, Bungay. *The Coaching Habit: Say Less, Ask More & Change the Way You Lead Forever.* Box of Crayons Press, 2016.

Stoltzfus, Tony. *Coaching Questions: A Coach's Guide to Powerful Asking Skills.* Coach22 Bookstore LLC, 2008.

Thompson, Henry. *Introduction to FIRO Element B in Organizations.* Wormhole Publishing, 2001.

Treasurer, Bill. *Leaders Open Doors, 2nd Edition: A Radically Simple Leadership Approach to Lift People, Profits, and Performance.* Association for Talent Development, 2015.

Whitmore, John. *Coaching for performance: GROWing human potential and purpose: the principles and practice of coaching and leadership. People skills for professionals (4th ed.).* Nicholas Brealey, 2009.

Wilson, Carol. *Best Practice in Performance Coaching: A Handbook for Leaders, Coaches, HR Professionals and Organizations.* Kogan Page, 2007.

ABOUT THE AUTHOR

Alonzo Johnson, Ph.D., is the author of the *Made Easy Series*, which features books titled *Coaching Made Easy, Leading Made Easy* and *Hiring Made Easy as PIE*. He is passionate about helping people grow professionally and fulfills this passion by coaching others and serving as Managing Partner of The OASYS Group, a talent management consulting company.

Alonzo possesses a unique array of experience, which he has gained while serving in the military, higher education, and in the private business sector. With expertise gained from over three decades honing his skills in staffing and organizational development, Alonzo has helped organizations to manage the talent and performance of their employees.

He specializes in coaching leaders to improve their effectiveness by creating and deploying leadership development initiatives. Alonzo leverages assessments as a foundation on which to build awareness and identify performance gaps. Alonzo has used this approach to help leaders at all levels to increase their leadership effectiveness.

The LEAD 360 and COACH[180] assessments, both developed by Alonzo, are companion leadership tools for *Leading Made Easy and Coaching Made Easy* respectively. Alonzo is also certified to administer and interpret the results of other value-added leadership development tools and assessments.

ABOUT THE OASYS GROUP

The OASYS Group is a talent management consulting company. The mission of the company is to *help people grow* by providing talent management solutions for every stage of employment—from recruiting and onboarding new employees to engaging, developing, and retaining existing employees. The OASYS Group's core strategy is to align performance management processes with business goals. The competency-based approach creates a synchronized work environment in which employees are engaged, thereby increasing performance and reducing turnover.

The OASYS Group's consultants are passionate about leadership development. They take an unusual, but systematic approach to developing leaders by leveraging three critical factors: assessment, assignment and association. These critical factors are articulated as the AAA model. First, assessments are administered to the leader and the results are used to identify opportunities for growth. Next, work assignments that will provide stretch-goals are explored and identified. This assignment can be leading a project team within the leader's current role, or serving in a different role altogether—as long as the assignment affords growth opportunities. And finally, leaders develop associations that provide coaching or mentoring in the areas identified for improvement.

Sometimes leaders require more individualized help to achieve their goals. The OASYS Group employs a variety of coaching tools and strategies to help leaders realize their goals.

www.ingramcontent.com/pod-product-compliance
Lightning Source LLC
Chambersburg PA
CBHW020652300426
44112CB00007B/340

9780986396564